iPad 8th Generation User Manual

The Ultimate Ridiculously Simple Guide to Master the New iPad 8th Generation

Kelly Newton

Contents

Introduction

You can make the new iPad 8 Generation your own and do a lot of useful things with it using well-structured detailed and step by step guide for non techies. You are going to learn how to personalize your iPad, Change the wallpaper on your Home Screen, add widgets, create your own Memoji, and set a Dark Mode schedule.

You will also learn intuitive gestures, use face unlock, and explore the limits of possibility with the amazing Ultra Wide camera. Capture great images with your iPad 8 Gen in any situation. Whether it's a casual photo to a studio-quality portrait—your iPad 8 Gen camera can do it.

Travel in ease with your iPad 8 Gen—scout locations in advance, check airport information, organize your credit cards and travel, and relive the memories when you return home.

Unlike other books, this guide comes with INDEX to help you look out for specific words or features that you might be interested in. Meaning you can easily look out for health, fitness, activity patterns, sleep routine and more.

So, are you ready? Let's dive right into the guide!

What's new in iPadOS 14

Here are list of the Exciting new features in the new iOS 14.

Home Screen Widgets

The first exciting new features we'll be looking at are those handy widgets on the home screen. If you've got an iOS 14, you now have the luxury of getting a lot of information at a glance as the widgets have been completely redesigned.

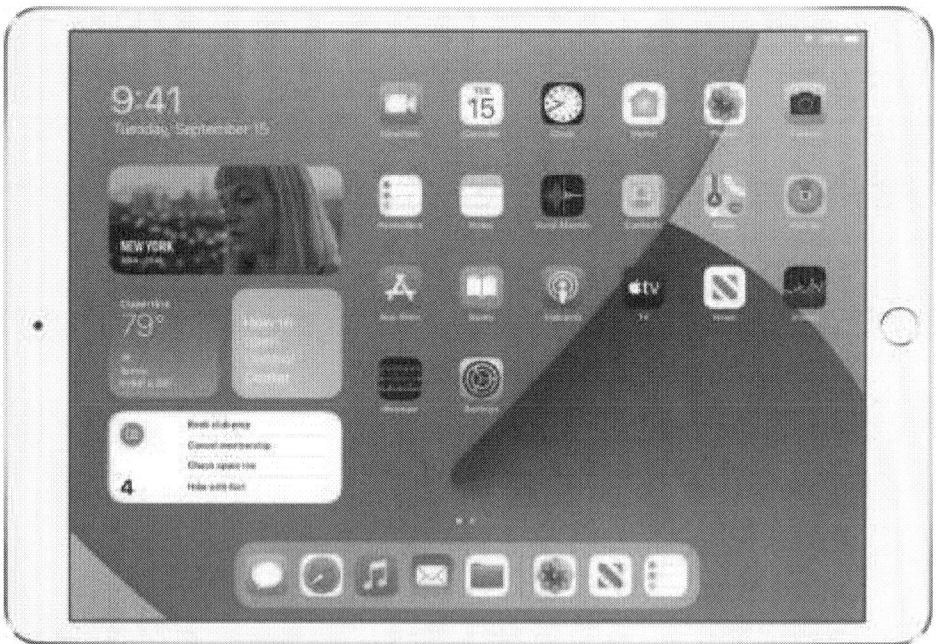

You have the option of choosing different sizes, arrange them in any manner and add them as part of your home screen. Exciting right? The cool thing is, there's also a smart stack option that allows you to classify and display your widgets based on certain parameters such as time, location or activity.

App Library Still on the home screen, there's a new app library that organizes all your apps into an easy to navigate view. Not only those, your apps are sorted into categories and the frequently used ones made just a click away.

Compact calls

Another cool feature in the new iOS 14 is that all your calls now appear with a design that doesn't take up the whole screen. This includes calls from supported third-party apps.

App clips

When you need a small part of an app to focus on specific tasks e.g ordering a meal or bike renting, App clip is your plug. It can be found in messages, safari, maps and even by scanning QR codes. Stick with us to learn how to go about it.

Translate Language

lovers are in for a swell time with the new Translate app. You can have conversations easily with this app by translating using voice or text. Simply put the orientation of your phone in landscape if you wish to enter a conversation mode.

You also have the option to download your favorite languages and save your favorite translations.

Search

This is not your regular search feature. On the new iOS 14, searching across the web, apps, and contacts now come in handy with an as-you type experience and sleek design. You get faster responses too.

Picture in Picture

If you wish to watch videos or do FaceTime call while you do something else on another app, the picture in picture feature allows you do that.

Messages

New features in the message app include directing a message to someone by mentioning them in a conversation and getting to an important message faster by pinning it to the top. In group conversations, you can now use inline replies also.

Memoji

Sounds like a combination of meme and emoji. You can now select from over 15 faces, age and hair options to reflect different personality and profession.

Maps

With maps, worry no more about directions and landmarks. Eateries, shops, great places and all can be easily discovered from the map feature consisting roads, paths and different lanes.

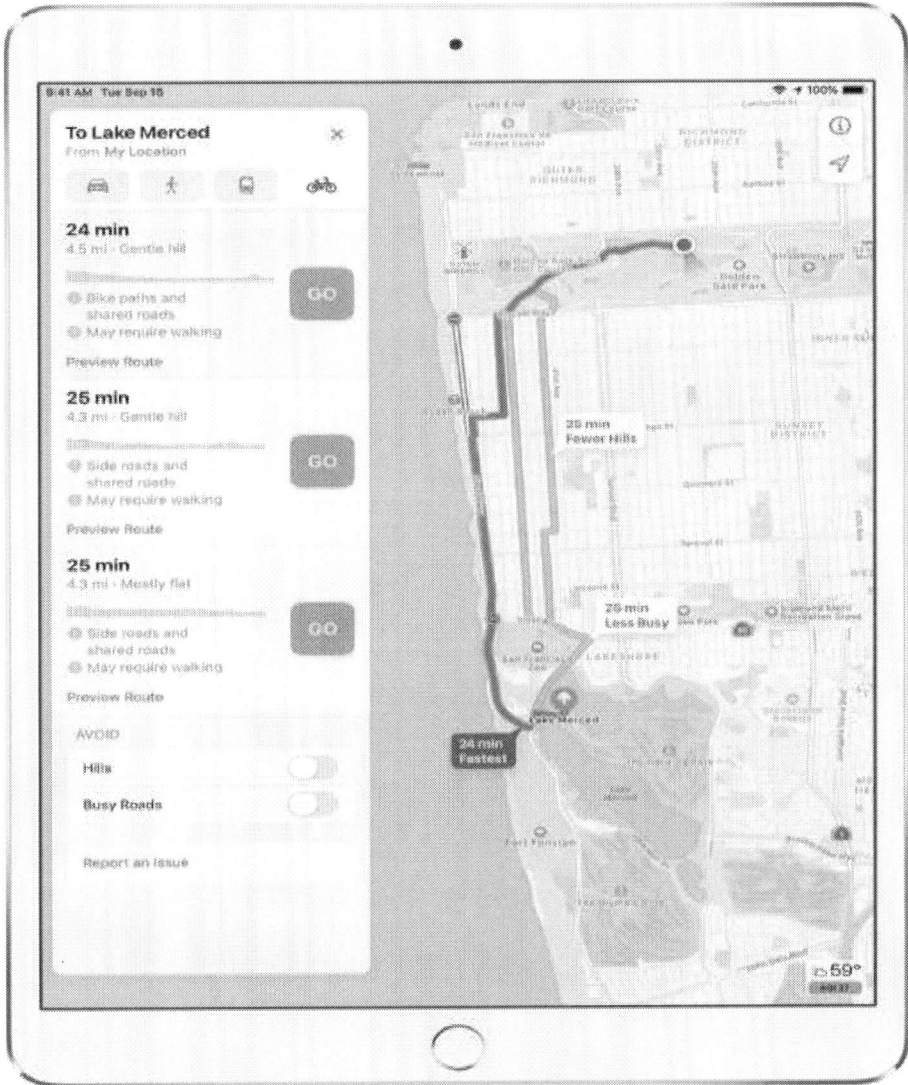

Camera

What have we got here? You can now easily change video frame rate and resolution by using quick toggles in video mode. If you've ever wanted to capture mirrored selfies which reflects front camera preview, now is your chance.

Photos

New features in photos allows you to add captions to your media items. Also available is the filter option as well as the ability to sort your photos by date.

Reminders

If you wish to share certain reminders with people you share list with, now you can do so. The feature also suggests times, dates or location based on past reminders. Cool right? It's a whole new dawn of organizing experience on iOS14

Siri

Siri keeps getting better with the new iOS14. It can now send audio messages, provide information across the Internet and many more just to help you get answers.

Safari

With its beta version, you can get a website translated to 7 different languages. If your password ain't secure enough, safari hints you in a jiffy. If you're also interested in how certain websites handle your privacy, worry no more. The new safari is simply a new level of security.

Health

Worried about sleep time and pattern? The health app is your new found solace. A checklist is also available if you need to activate other features in the app.

Headphone Sound

Level You can do two major things among many other features here; setting your desired audio level while playing something and even setting volume limits.

FaceTime

when you're looking at the screen, the new feature helps you maintain eye contact during video calls. Also, people using sign languages can now be detected and made prominent to give a more exciting and hitchfree communication experience.

Home

What have we got here? If you've tagged someone in your photo app, doorbells and video cameras can now identify those people. This is nothing less than cool. You can also use adaptive lighting throughout the day to adjust lighting levels. One more thing; in set activity zones, you can be given an alert if motion is detected.

Car keys

No excuse for losing your car keys anymore as you can now use a digital key by just bringing your phone near the car door to unlock. Start your car by placing your phone on a wireless charger or reader and you're set. If you wish to share the digital key with a third party, be our guest. Customizing control for various drivers is another exciting feature on your new iOS. .

CarPlay

This new feature now supports more app types such as meal ordering, charging for electric vehicles and many more. You also have the luxury of checking out and choosing from many exciting wallpapers.

Privacy

Everyone loves a little bit of privacy. Whenever an app is using your cameras or microphone, you'll be duly notified through an indicator on the top of your screen. This feature vary depending on your region, carrier, language and phone model. You can now also share approximate locations with apps.

If you're excited about these scintillating features, let's move on to how to use and go around them.

Chapter 1: Turn On and Set Up iPad 8 Gen

You can turn on and set up your iPad 8 Gen over the internet or you can decide to set it up by connecting it to a computer. You can also transfer your data to your new iPad 8 Gen, or Android device.

Note: If your iPad 8 Gen is deployed or managed by another company or organization, you have to see an administrator for setup instructions.

Prepare For Setup

You need the following items for a hitch free setup:

- An Internet connection, Wi-Fi network (you might need the name and password of the network) or cellular data service through a carrier.
- Your Apple ID and password; if you don't have one, you can create it during setup
- Your credit or debit card account information, in case you'd like to add a card to Apple Pay during setup
- Your previous iPad 8 Gen or a backup of your device, if you want to transfer your data to your new device
- If you are transferring from an Android, then you need the Android device.

Turn On and Set Up Your iPad 8 Gen

1. Press and hold the top button until you see the Apple logo displayed.

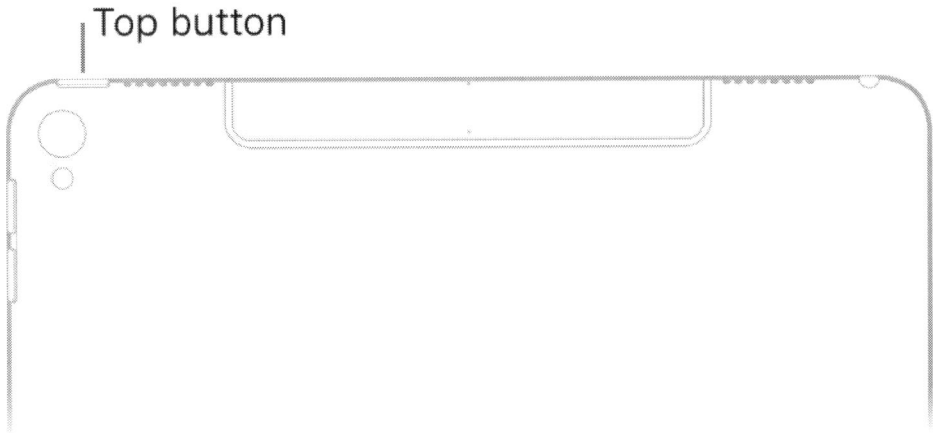

Top button

If iPad 8 Gen doesn't turn on, it's possible that the battery is low, charge it.

Do one of the following:

- Tap Set Up Manually, then follow the setup instructions on your screen.

- In case you have another iPad 8 Gen, iPhone, or iPod touch with iOS 11 or a later version, you may use Quick Start to automatically set up your new device. You will have to bring the two devices close together, then follow the instructions on your screen to securely copy many of your settings, preferences, and iCloud Keychain.

- Then, you can restore the rest of your data and content to your new iPad 8 Gen from your iCloud backup.

Or, if iOS 12.4 or later is installed on both devices, you can transfer all your data wirelessly from your previous device to your new one. Keep the devices near each other and connect them to a power source until the migration process is complete.

You can also use wired connection to transfer your data between the devices.

- If you have low vision or are blind, triple-click the Home button to turn on VoiceOver app, the screen reader.

Move from an Android Device to iPad 8 Gen

You can also automatically and securely move your files from an Android device, when you set up your device.

Note: you can only use the Move to iOS app when you first set up your iPad 8 Gen. If you have already set up your device you have to move your data manually, but if you still want to use the Move to iOS app, then you must erase your iPad 8 Gen and restart the set-up.

1. You can only use this on devices with Android version 4.0 or later,

2. On your iPad 8 Gen:

a. Follow the setup assistant.

b. Then select Move Data from Android on the Apps & Data screen.

3. On the Android device:

12

a. Turn on Wi-Fi.

b. Open the Move to iOS app.

c. Follow the instructions on your screen.

Set Up Cellular Service on iPad 8 Gen

You need a SIM card to use cellular connection on your iPad 8 Gen, contact your carrier to set up a cellular plan.

These are some of the ways you can use Dual SIM:

- Use one number for business and another one for personal calls.
- Add a local data plan whenever you travel to a different region.
- Have separate subscriptions for voice and data plans.

Note: you need to unlock your iPad 8 Gen before you can use two different carriers.

Install the Nano-SIM

1. Insert a SIM eject tool or paper clip into the small hole of your SIM tray, then push in toward the iPad 8 Gen to eject the tray.

SIM tray

Paper clip or
SIM eject tool

2. Remove the tray from your iPad 8 Gen.

3. Put the nano-SIM in the tray. Follow the angled corner to get the correct orientation.

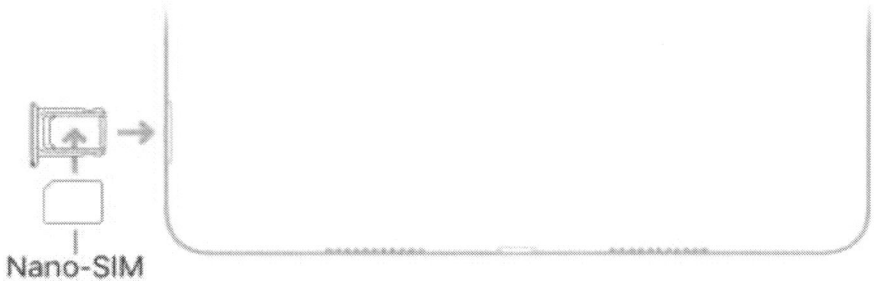

Nano-SIM

4. Insert the tray back into your iPad 8 Gen.

5. If there is a PIN on the nano-SIM, carefully enter it when prompted.

WARNING: Don't ever try to guess the PIN of a SIM card. If your guess is incorrect, the sim may be locked permanently, then you would be unable to make or receive calls or use cellular data through you carrier until you buy a new SIM.

 Important: You will probably need a nano-SIM to use cellular service, when you connect to GSM networks and CDMA networks.

If you activate your iPad 8 Gen on a CDMA wireless network, you can still use a nano-SIM to connect to a GSM network, especially for international roaming.

The policies of your wireless service provider will affect your iPad 8 Gen, this may include restriction on roaming and switching service providers, even after you conclude a required minimum service contract.

For more information, contact your wireless service provider. The availability of cellular reception will depend on the model of your iPad 8 Gen, the wireless network and your location.

Set Up Your Cellular Plan With Esim

If your iPad 8 Gen supports eSIM, the eSIM provided by your carrier will be stored digitally in the iPad 8 Gen.

1. Open Settings ⚙ > Cellular, then tap Add Cellular Plan.

2. Place your iPad 8 Gen so that the QR code provided by your carrier appears in the frame, or you can enter the details manually. You might be required to enter a confirmation code provided by your carrier.

3. Tap Add Cellular Plan.

4. If the new plan is your second line, follow the instructions on your screen to set the way the plans should work.

You can also activate your cellular plan through your carrier's app, if the option is supported. Open the App Store and download your carrier's app, then you can use the app to activate a cellular plan. Although you can store more than one eSIM on your iPad 8 Gen, you can't use more than one at a time. If you want to switch the eSIM, go to Settings > Cellular, tap the plan you want,   then tap Turn On This Line. You can use a nano-SIM as your second line.

Manage Your Cellular Plans

When setting up a model that supports Dual SIM, you can select how iPad 8 Gen uses each line. Follow this if you want to change the setting later:

1. Go to Settings ⚙ > Cellular.

2. Do the following:

a. Tap Cellular Data, then select a default line. Turn on Allow Cellular Data Switching to allow iPad 8 Gen to use either line depending on coverage and availability.

If you are outside of the region covered by the carrier network and Data Roaming is on, you will incur roaming charges.

b. Tap Default Voice Line, then select a line.

c. Below Cellular Plans, tap a line, then change settings such as SIM PIN, Cellular Plan Label, Wi-Fi Calling (if available from your carrier), or Calls on Other Devices. You will see the label in Phone, Messages, and Contacts.

Note the following when using Dual SIM:

You have to turn on Wi-Fi Calling on a line if you want to use that line to receive calls while the other line is on a call.

If Wi-Fi connection is unavailable and you receive a call on one line while the other is on a call, iPad 8 Gen will use the cellular data of the line that is on the call to receive a call on the other line.

You may be charged for this. If you want to receive a call on the other line, you have to permit the line that is on the call for data use in Cellular Data Settings (either as your default line or as the non-default line with Allow Cellular Data Switching turned on).

If Wi-Fi calling is not turned on for a line and one line is on a call, incoming phone calls on the other line (including calls from emergency services) will directly go to voicemail (if it is available on your carrier) and you won't be notified about the missed call.

You can enable conditional call forwarding (if available from your carrier) from one line to another when a line is busy or not in service, to prevent calls from going to voicemail; your carrier can provide more information on this.

- Any call you make from another device, for example, your Mac, by relaying it through your iPad 8 Gen with Dual SIM, the default voice line will be used for this call.

- You can't switch an SMS/MMS Messages conversation from one line to another, once started: you have to delete the conversation and restart it with the other line.

- Note that additional charges will incur, if you send SMS/MMS attachments on a line without selecting it for cellular data.

- The line selected for cellular data will be used for instant Hotspot and Personal Hotspot.

- You should consider applicable voice, data and roaming charges when you are managing your cellular plans, particularly when travelling with your iPad 8 Gen.
- For some carriers, you will be able to unlock iPad 8 Gen for use with another carrier (additional fees may apply). For authorization and setup information, contact your carrier.

Connect iPad 8 Gen to the Internet

Yes, it is time to connect your iPad 8 Gen to the Internet by using available cellular or Wi-Fi network. To do that:

1. Open Settings > Wi-Fi, then turn on Wi-Fi.

2. Tap one of the following:

• A network: if a password is required, enter it.

• Others: Join a hidden network. Enter the name, security type, and password of the hidden network.

If the iPad 8 Gen is connected to a Wi-Fi network the Wi-Fi icon will be displayed at the top of the screen (open Safari and view a webpage to verify this), your iPad 8 Gen will reconnect whenever you return to the location.

Connect iPad 8 Gen to a Cellular Network

If a Wi-Fi network is unavailable, iPad 8 Gen automatically connects to your carrier's cellular data. Check the following if your iPad 8 Gen doesn't connect:

1. Check if your SIM is activated and unlocked.

2. Open Settings > Cellular.

3. Ensure you turned on your Cellular Data. For Dual SIM models, tap Cellular Data, then verify the selected line. (You only choose one line for cellular data.)

If you need an Internet connection, the iPad 8 Gen will do the following in the listed order, until a connection is made:

• Try to connect to the last used available Wi-Fi network

• Show all Wi-Fi networks within range and connect to any one of your choice.

• Try connecting to your carrier's cellular data network

Note: If apps and services can't connect to the internet over a Wi-Fi network, they may transfer data over to your carrier's cellular network (additional charges will incur). For more information on your cellular data plan rates, contact your carrier.

Manage Apple ID and iCloud Settings on iPad 8 Gen

You will need your Apple ID to access Apple services such as the App Store, the iTunes Store, Apple Music, FaceTime, Icloud, Apple Books, iMessage, and more.

Store and secure your photos, videos, documents, music, apps, and more— on iCloud, and keep them updated across all your devices. iCloud makes it easy for you to share photos, calendars, locations, and more, with friends and family. You can also use it to find your iPad 8 Gen, if you lose it.

On iCloud, you get a free email account and 5 GB of storage for your mail, documents, photos and videos, and backups. The music, apps, TV shows, and books, you buy doesn't count against your available storage space. You can also upgrade your iCloud storage from iPad 8 Gen.

Note: Minimum system requirements will affect some iCloud features. The availability of iCloud will differ according to your location or country.

Sign in with your Apple ID

Do the following if you did not sign in during setup:

1. Open Settings .

2. Select Sign in to your iPad 8 Gen.

3. Enter your Apple ID and password.

You can create an Apple ID, if you don't have one.

4. Enter the six-digit pin if you protect your account with two-factor authentication.

Visit the Recover on your Apple ID website if you forget your password.

Change your Apple ID settings

1. Open Settings and go to [your name].

2. Use any of the following:

• Update your contact information

• Change your password

• Manage Family Sharing

Change your iCloud settings

1. Open Settings > [your name] > iCloud.

2. Do any of these

• See your iCloud storage status.

• To upgrade your iCloud storage—tap Manage Storage > Change Storage Plan.

• Turn on the features you want, such as Photos, Mail, Contacts, and Messages.

Ways to use iCloud on iPad 8 Gen

Keep these contents up to date:

- Contact, Mail, Messages, Calendars, Notes, and Reminders
- Photos and videos;
- Music, books and apps;
- Documents;
- Bookmarks, the webpages you open in Safari and your reading list;
- Passwords and credit cards;

You can also do these:

- View your iCloud data on your iPad 8 Gen, iPhone, iPod touch, Mac, Apple Watch, and iCloud.com (with a Mac or a Windows PC).
- Choose people you want to share your photos and videos with.
- Have iCloud storage plans of over 200 GB and share with up to six family members.

- Locate any missing iPad 8 Gen, iPhone, iPod touch, Mac, Apple Watch or AirPods belonging to you or any member of your family.
- Find your friends and family; share locations between family and friends, so that you can find each other on a map.
- Backup and restore your data.

Note: you can't use iTunes to sync apps such as Music, Photos, Calendar, and Contacts with your computer if you enable iCloud for them.

Wake and unlock iPad 8 Gen

To save power, iPad 8 Gen turns off the display, locks for security, and goes to sleep when not in use. iPad 8 Gen will wake and unlock quickly when you want to use it.

Wake iPad 8 Gen

Do any of the following to wake your iPad 8 Gen:

• Press the top button.

Top button

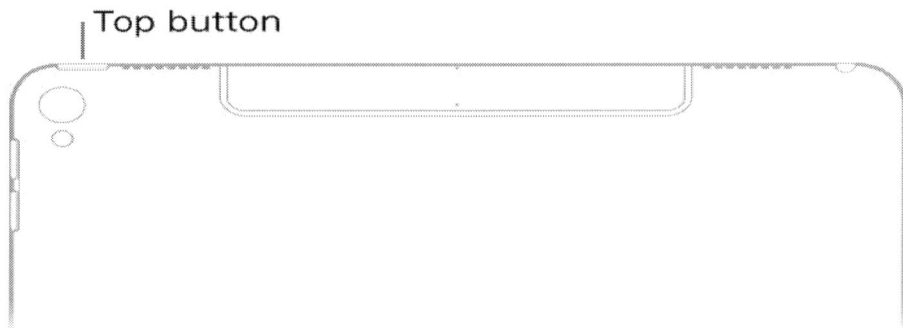

Tap the screen. Tap the screen with Apple

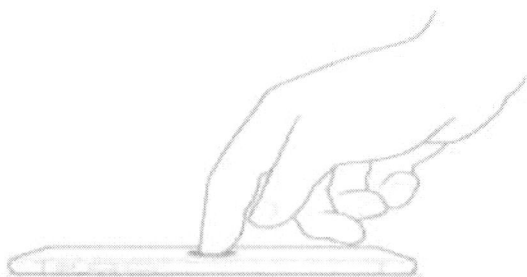

How to Unlock iPad 8 Gen with Face ID

1. To wake your iPad 8 Gen, tap the screen or raise iPad 8 Gen, then glance at it.

To indicate that your iPad 8 Gen is unlocked, the lock icon animates from closed to open.

2. Swipe up on the screen.

Press the side button to lock your iPad 8 Gen. If you don't touch the screen for a minute or more, iPad 8 Gen will lock automatically.

How to Unlock iPad 8 Gen with Touch ID (Modes that have a Home button)

Use the finger you registered on Touch ID to press the Home button.

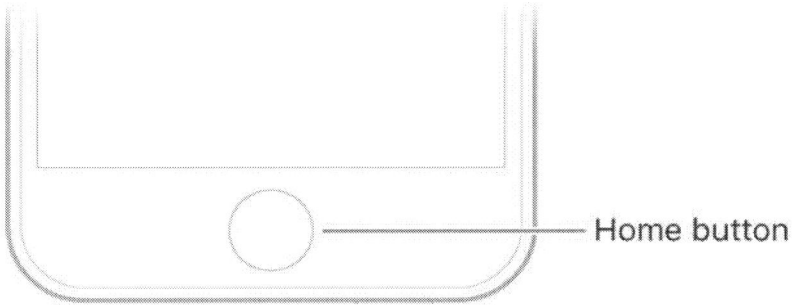
Home button

Press the side button or Sleep/Wake button (depending on your model) to lock iPad 8 Gen again. If you don't touch the screen for about a minute or more, iPad 8 Gen locks automatically.

Unlock iPad 8 Gen with A Passcode

1. Swipe upward on the Lock screen

2. Enter your passcode.

Press the side button or Sleep/Wake button (depending on your model), to lock iPad 8 Gen again. If you don't touch the screen for about a minute or more, iPad 8 Gen locks automatically.

Chapter 2: Learn Basic Gestures to interact with iPad 8 Gen

Use a few simple gestures such as—tap, touch and hold, swipe, scroll, and zoom to control your iPad 8 Gen.

Tap: Using one finger, touch the screen lightly.

Touch and hold: To preview contents and perform quick actions, in an app or Control Center, touch and hold them. Touch and hold any app icon briefly on the Home screen, to open a quick action menu.

Swipe: Quickly move one finger across the screen.

Scroll: Move a finger across the screen without lifting it. For instance, in Photos, drag a list up or down to see more. Swipe to scroll quickly, then touch the screen to stop scrolling.

Zoom: Place two fingers near each other on your screen. Then try to move them towards each other to zoom out or try taking the fingers away from each other to zoom in. You will need to Double-tap a photo or webpage to zoom in, then double-tap again to zoom out.

In Maps, double-tap and hold, then drag down to zoom out or drag up to zoom in.

Learn Gestures for New iPad 8 Gen

Here's a brief reference to the gestures you can use to interact with New iPad 8 Gen.

Go Home: To return to the Home screen at any time, swipe up from the bottom of your screen.

Quickly access controls: To open , swipe down from the top-right corner of your screen; touch and hold a control to reveal more options. If you want to add or remove items, open Settings > Control Center > Customize Controls.

Open the App Switcher: Swipe up from the bottom edge of your screen, pause at the center, then lift your finger. Swipe right to browse the open apps, then tap the app you want to use.

Switch between open apps: To quickly switch between apps, Swipe right or left along the bottom edge of the screen.

Ask Siri. Say, "Hey Siri." You can also hold down the side button, then make your request. Until you release the button, Siri will listen.

Use Apple Pay: To view your default credit card, double-click the side button, authenticate with Face ID by glancing at iPad 8 Gen.

Use Accessibility Shortcut: Triple-click the side button.

Take a screenshot. Press and quickly release the side button and volume up button, simultaneously.

Use Emergency SOS   (all regions except India): Press and hold both the side button and either volume button simultaneously until the sliders appear, then drag Emergency SOS.

Use Emergency SOS (in India): Triple-click the side button or if Accessibility Shortcut is turned on, press and hold the side button and either volume button simultaneously, until the sliders appear, then drag Emergency SOS.

Turn off: Press and hold the side button and either volume button simultaneously, until the liders appear, then drag the top slider to power off. Or go to Settings > General > Shut Down.

Force restart: Press and release the volume up button, press and release the volume down button, then press and hold the side button until the Apple logo is displayed.

View Previews and Quick actions Menus On IPad 8 Gen

On the Home screen, in apps and Control Center, you can check previews, open quick actions menus, and more.

See Previews and Quick Actions Menus

• Touch and hold an image in the Photo app, to preview it and see a list of options.

• Touch and hold a message in your mailbox, in the Mail app, to preview the message contents and see a list of options.

• (If the icons start to jiggle, press the Home button or tap Done at the top right.

• Open Control Center, then touch and hold an item such as brightness controls or Camera to see options.

• Touch and hold a notification, on the lock screen to respond to it.

• Touch and hold the Spacebar with one finger, when typing, to turn your keyboard into a trackpad.

Explore the iPad 8 Gen Home screen and open apps

Explore the Home screen and apps on your iPad 8 Gen. All your apps will be organized into pages on the Home screen. When space is needed for more apps, pages will be added.

1. Swipe up from the bottom edge of the screen.

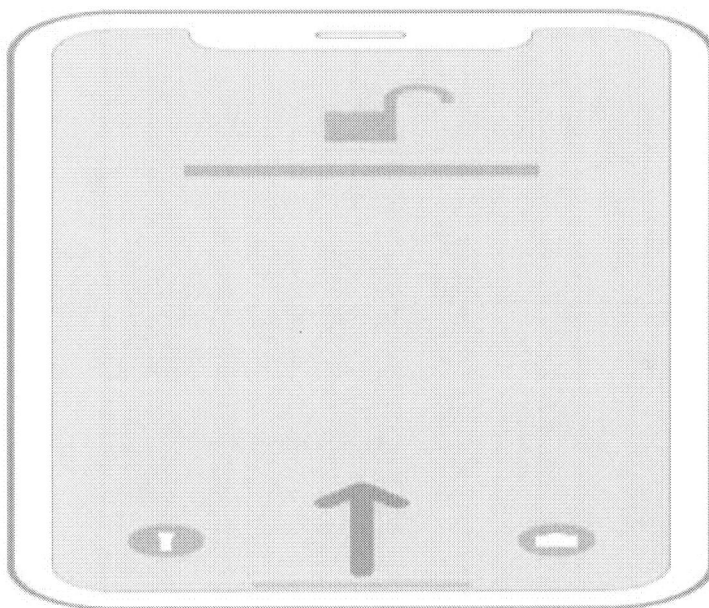

2. Swipe right or left to browse apps on other Home screen pages.

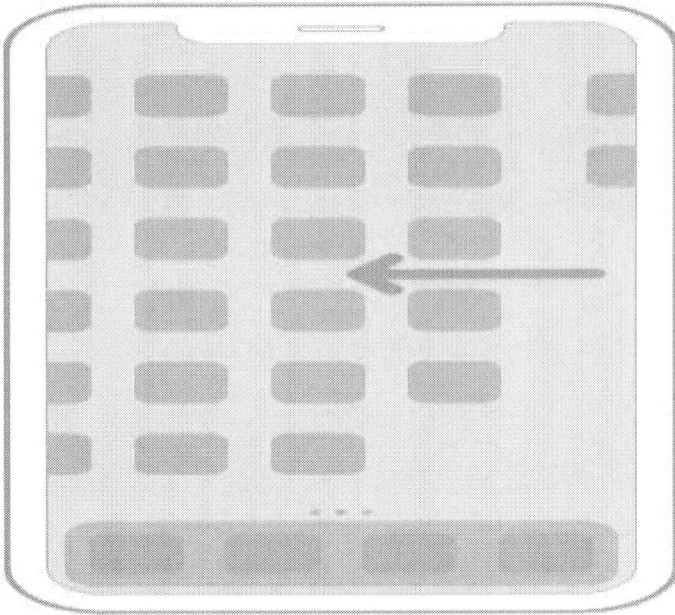

3. Tap any app icon on the Home screen to it.

4. Swipe up from the bottom edge of the screen. You can also move, remove, or organize apps.

Change Common iPad 8 Gen Settings

You can configure and customize your iPad 8 Gen with Settings (located on the Home screen). You can change your iPad 8 Gen's name, set your language and region, choose different sounds for notifications among others. Information about common settings and their location is provided below.

Tap Settings to change your iPhone settings (volume, display brightness, and more).

Find Settings

Open Settings, then swipe down to reveal the search field, enter a term such as—"alert" or   password," then tap a setting.

Set the Date and Time

The time and date, visible on the Lock screen, are set automatically based on your location. You can adjust them if they're incorrect.

1. Open Settings > General, then tap Date & Time.

2. Turn on either of these:

• **Set Automatically:** correct time will be gotten from your network and updated for your time zone. This will not work for networks that don't support network time.

• **24-Hour Time:** (only available for some regions) the hours will be displayed from 0 to 23.

• Turn off Set Automatically, then change the date and time, to change the default date and time.

Set the Language and Region

1. Open Settings > General > Language & Region.

2. Set the following:

• The language for your iPad 8 Gen

• Your region

• The format of the calendar

• The unit of temperature (Celsius or Fahrenheit)

3. If you want to add a keyboard for another language, open Settings > General > Keyboard > Keyboards, then tap Add New Keyboard.

Change the Name of Your iPad 8 Gen

iTunes, iCloud, AirDrop, and Personal Hotspot use the name of your iPad 8 Gen.

1. Open Settings, then tap General > About > Name.

2. Tap the Clear Text button, enter the new name, then tap Done.

Set Up Mail, Contacts, and Calendar Accounts

iPad 8 Gen works with much more apps than the ones that came with it and those you use on iCloud. It works with Microsoft Exchange and most popular Internet-based mail, contacts, and calendar services.

1. Open Settings > Passwords & Accounts > Add Account.

2. Tap an email service to enter it such as—Google, Yahoo, or Aol.com—then enter your email account information.

3. Tap Other, then do the following, to add contacts or calendar account:

• To add a contact account: Tap Add LDAP Account or Add CardDAV Account (if supported by your company or organization), then enter your details;

• To add a calendar account: Tap Add CalDAV Account, then input your information;

• To subscribe to iCal (.ics) calendars: Tap Add Subscribed Calendar, then enter the URL of the .ics file to subscribe to; or import an .ics file from your Mail.

33

Chapter 3: Change or Lock the Screen Orientation on iPad 8 Gen

Some apps have different layouts when used in landscape orientation. These include Mail, Photos, Messages, and Calendar.

Note: if Display Zoom is enabled, these different layouts won't be available.

Lock or Unlock the Screen Orientation

Lock the screen orientation to prevent it from changing when you rotate iPad 8 Gen.

1. Go to Control Center, then tap the Lock Orientation button 🔒.

2. When the Lock Orientation icon 🔒 appears in the status bar, then the screen orientation is locked.

Change the wallpaper on iPad 8 Gen

You can choose a photo or image as wallpaper for the Lock screen or Home screen, on iPad 8 Gen. You can choose from stills or dynamic.

Change the Wallpaper

1. Open Settings > Wallpaper > Choose a New Wallpaper.

2. Do one of these:

• Choose a preset image from a group at the top of your screen (Stills and dynamic, and so on).

Wallpaper marked with the appearance button ◉ will change, when you turn on Dark mode.

- Choose one fro your photos (tap an album, then tap the photo).To reposition a chosen image, pinch open to zoom in, drag it with your finger to move it.   Now, Pinch close to zoom out.

3. Tap Set, then select one of these:

- Set Lock Screen
- Set Home Screen
- Set Both

Set A Live Photo As Wallpaper For The Lock Screen

If you set a Live Photo as your wallpaper, play the Live photo by pressing the Lock screen.

1. Open Settings > Wallpaper > Choose a New Wallpaper.

2. Do one of these:

- Tap Live, then choose a Live Photo.
- Open your Live Photos album, then select a Live Photo (It may take a while to download).

3. Tap Set, then select Set Lock Screen or Set Both.

Adjust the iPad 8 Gen Screen Brightness and Color

On iPad 8 Gen, dim the screen to extend battery life, use Night Shift, set Dark Mode, and automatically adjust the screen for your lighting conditions.

Turn Dark Mode on or off

Dark Mode gives the entire iPad 8 Gen experience a dark color scheme that's perfect for low-light environments. You can turn on Dark Mode from Control Center or set it to turn on automatically at night (or on a custom schedule) in Settings.

With Dark Mode turned on, you can use your iPad 8 Gen while, for example, reading in bed, without disturbing the person next to you.

Do any of the following:

- Open Control Center, touch and hold the Brightness button, then tap the Appearance button to turn Dark Mode on or off.
- Go to Settings > Display & Brightness, then select Dark to turn on Dark Mode, or select Light to turn it off.

Schedule Dark Mode to Turn On and Off Automatically

1. Go to Settings > Display & Brightness.

2. Turn on Automatic, then tap Options.

3. Select either Sunset to Sunrise or Custom Schedule.

If you choose Custom Schedule, tap the options to schedule the times you want Dark Mode to turn on and off.

If you select Sunset to Sunrise, iPad 8 Gen uses the data from your clock and geolocation to determine when it's nighttime for you.

Adjust the Screen Brightness Manually

To make your iPad 8 Gen screen dimmer or brighter, do one of the following:

- Open Control Center, then drag the Brightness button.

- Go to Settings > Display & Brightness, then drag the slider.

Adjust the Screen Brightness Automatically

iPad 8 Gen adjusts the screen brightness for current light conditions using the built-in ambient light sensor.

1. Go to Settings > Accessibility.

2. Tap Display & Text Size, then turn on Auto-Brightness.

Turn True Tone on or off

Turn on True Tone to automatically adapt to the color and intensity of the display to match the light in your environment.

Do any of the following:

- Open Control Center, touch and hold the Brightness button, then tap the True Tone button to turn True Tone on or off.
- Go to Settings > Display & Brightness, then turn True Tone on or off.

Turn Night Shift on or off

You can turn on Night Shift manually, which is helpful when you're in a darkened room during the day.

Open Control Center, touch and hold the Brightness button, then tap the Night Shift button.

Schedule Night Shift to turn on and off automatically

Use Night Shift to shift the colors in your display to the warmer end of the spectrum at night and make viewing the screen easier on your eyes.

1. Go to Settings > Display & Brightness > Night Shift.

2. Turn on Scheduled.

3. To adjust the color balance for Night Shift, drag the slider below Color Temperature toward the warmer or cooler end of the spectrum.

4. Then select either Sunset to Sunrise or Custom Schedule.

5. If you choose Custom Schedule, tap the options to schedule the times you want Night Shift to turn on and off.

If you select Sunset to Sunrise, iPad 8 Gen uses the data from your clock and geolocation to determine when it's nighttime for you.

Note: The Sunset to Sunrise option isn't available if you turned off Location Services in Settings > Privacy, or if you turned off Setting Time Zone in Settings > Privacy > Location Services > System Services.

Magnify the iPad 8 Gen Screen with Display Zoom

You can magnify what's on your screen, if your model supports this.

1. Open Settings > Display & Brightness.

2. Tap View, below Display Zoom.

3. Select Zoomed, then tap Set.

Bring screen items within reach on iPad 8 Gen

Bring items down to the lower half of your screen from the top, with Reachability.

Take a Screenshot or Screen Recording On iPad 8 Gen

Take a shot of your screen, as it is displayed, or record actions on your screen, then use it in documents or share with others.

Take a Screenshot

1. Do one of these:

● Press the side button and volume up button simultaneously, then release them.

Your screenshots will be saved in the Screenshots album of your Photos app, or in All Photos Album if you turned on iCloud Photos in Settings > Photos.

Tip: You can create a PDF of a document, email, or webpage, take a screenshot, tap the thumbnail, then tap Full Page.

Create a Screen Recording

Capture sound and create a screen recording on your iPad 8 Gen.

1. Open Settings > Control Center > Customize Controls, then tap the Insert button near the Screen Recording.

2. Go to Control Center, tap the Screen Recording button, then hold-on for three seconds.

3. If you want to stop a recording, open the Control Center, tap the red status bar at the top of your screen or the Selected Screen Recording button, then tap Stop.

Open Photos, then select your screen recording.

Adjust the volume on iPad 8 Gen

Use the buttons on the side of your iPad 8 Gen to adjust the audio volume when you're on the phone or watching a movie, listening to music or other media. The buttons also controls the volume for sound effects including alerts, ringers. You can also turn up or down the volume using Siri.

Ask Siri. Tell Siri something similar to, "Turn down the volume" or "Turn up the volume."

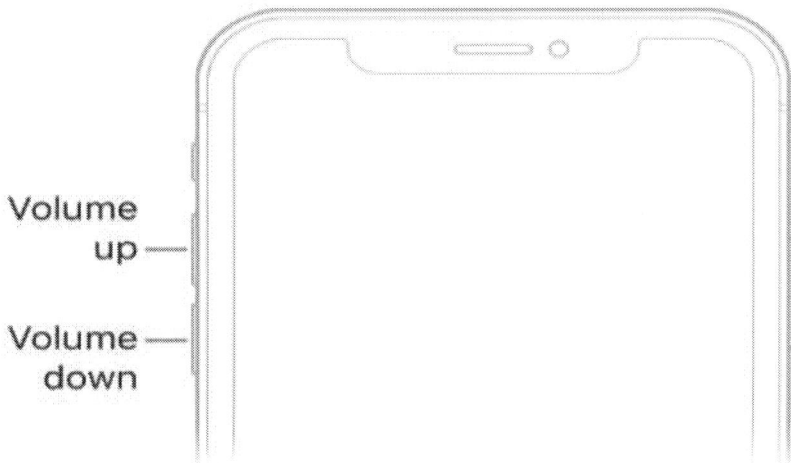

Volume
up —

Volume —
down

Lock the Ringer and Alert Volumes in Settings

1. Go to Settings.

2. Tap Sounds or Sounds & Haptics.

3. Switch Change with Buttons, off.

Adjust the volume in Control Center

You can adjust the volume in Control Center when iPad 8 Gen is locked or when you're using an app.

Go to Control Center, then drag the volume slider.

Limit the volume for music and videos

1. Open Settings > Music > Volume Limit.

2. Drag the slider until you reach the maximum volume level you desire.

Temporarily silence calls, alerts, and notifications

Go to Control Center, then tap the Do Not Disturb button.

Put iPad 8 Gen In Ring Or Silent Mode

Flip the Ring/Silent switch to put the iPad 8 Gen in either ring mode or silent mode.

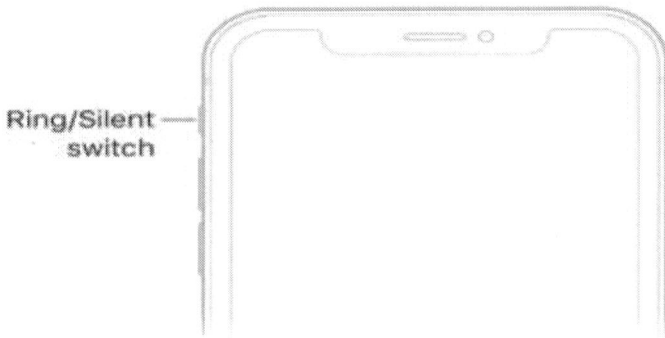

Ring/Silent switch

iPad 8 Gen will play all sounds in ring mode. iPad 8 Gen may only vibrate and not ring or play alerts and any other sound effects, in silent mode (the switch shows orange).

Important: Even when iPad 8 Gen is in silent mode, audio apps like Music, games and Clock alarms, play sound through the built-in speaker.

Sound effects for Camera, Voice Memos, and Emergency Alerts are played in some regions, even when the Ring/Silent switch is set to silent.

Change iPad 8 Gen Sounds and Vibrations

Visit Settings, to change the sounds iPad 8 Gen plays when you receive a text, call, email, voicemail, reminder, or other type of notification.

If your model supports it, you can feel the tap (called haptic feedback) when you perform some actions, like if you touch and hold the Camera icon on your Home screen.

Set Sound and Vibration Options

1. Open Settings > Sounds & Haptics.

2. Drag the slider below Ringers and Alerts to set the volume for all sounds.

3. Tap a sound type like ringtone or text tone, to set the tone and vibration patterns.

4. Do any of these:

• Select a tone (scroll to see all options).

Ringtones play for clock alarms, clock timer, and incoming calls; text tones will be used for new voicemail, text messages and other alerts.

• Tap Vibration, then choose a vibration pattern, or you can tap Create New Vibration to make your own.

Turn Haptic Feedback Off Or On

1. Go to Settings > Sounds & Haptics.

2. Switch System Haptics off or on.

Tip: If you cannot see and hear expected incoming calls and alerts at the right time, go to Control Center, then check if Do Not Disturb is on.

Tap the Do Not Disturb button to turn it off, if it is highlighted. (The Do Not Disturb icon will appear on your status bar, when it is turned on).

Chapter 4: Change Notification Settings on iPad 8 Gen

In Settings, set up location based alerts, change alert sound, choose which app can send notifications, allow government alerts, and more.

Change Notification Settings

Choose where you want notifications to be displayed, have notifications play a sound, turn off notifications from specific apps, among others.

1. Open Settings > Notifications.

2. Tap Show Previews, then select an option, to choose when to display notification previews.

If you choose When Unlocked, previews will also be displayed on the Lock screen. Previews include invitation details (from Calendar) and texts (from Mail or Messages).

3. To turn notification on or off, tap Back, then tap the app below Notification Style, then turn Allow Notifications on or off.

After turning on notification, choose where or how you want them to be displayed such as in the Notification Center or on your Lock screen.

4. Tap Notification Grouping, then choose how you want to group your notifications:

• By App: group every notification from a single app together.

- Automatic: group the notifications according to an organizing criteria supplied by the app, for example thread or topic.
- Off: Turn grouping off.

If you want to turn off notifications for any app, go to Settings > Notifications > Siri Suggestions, then turn off the app.

Show Recent Notifications on the Lock Screen

To allow access to Notification Center from the Lock screen.

1. Open Settings > Face ID & Passcode

2. Input your passcode.

3. Turn on the Notification Center

Silence All Your Notifications

Ask Siri. Say a request similar to: "Turn on Do Not Disturb."

Or open Settings > Do Not Disturb, then turn on Do Not Disturb.

Set Up Location based Alerts

Some apps will send alerts relevant to your location. Such as a reminder to call someone when leaving for your next location or when you get there.

You can turn off this type of alerts, if you don't want them.

1. Open Settings > Privacy > Location Services.

2. Turn Location Services on.

3. Tap an app, then choose if you'd like to share your location with the app.

Get Government Alerts

You can turn on Government alerts in some regions. In the US, for example, you can receive presidential alerts, the Emergency (both Severe and Extreme Imminent Threat alert), Public Safety and Amber Alerts are on by default. Turn them off, if you'd prefer.

You can receive Emergency Earthquake Alerts from the Japan Meteorological Agency on your iPad 8 Gen, in Japan.

1. Open Settings > Notifications.

2. Scroll down to the Government Alerts section, then turn on anyone you want.

Government alerts will differ depending on the model of your iPad 8 Gen or your carrier, and they may not work in some conditions.

Set Do Not Disturb on iPad 8 Gen

If you are going to have a dinner night with a special someone, you can silence your phone by turning on Do Not Disturb. Calls and notifications will be silenced and they won't light up your screen.

Turn on Do Not Disturb

Ask Siri. Say anything similar to: "Turn off Do Not Disturb," or "Turn on Do Not Disturb."

1. You can also turn on, Do Not Disturb by going to the Control Center, then tap the Do Not Disturb icon.

2. The Do Not Disturb icon will be displayed in the status bar, if you turn on, Do Not Disturb. Touch and hold the Do Not Disturb icon in Control Center, then choose an option, if you want to set an ending time for Do Not Disturb. Another option is to tap Schedule, turn on Scheduled, then set beginning and ending times.

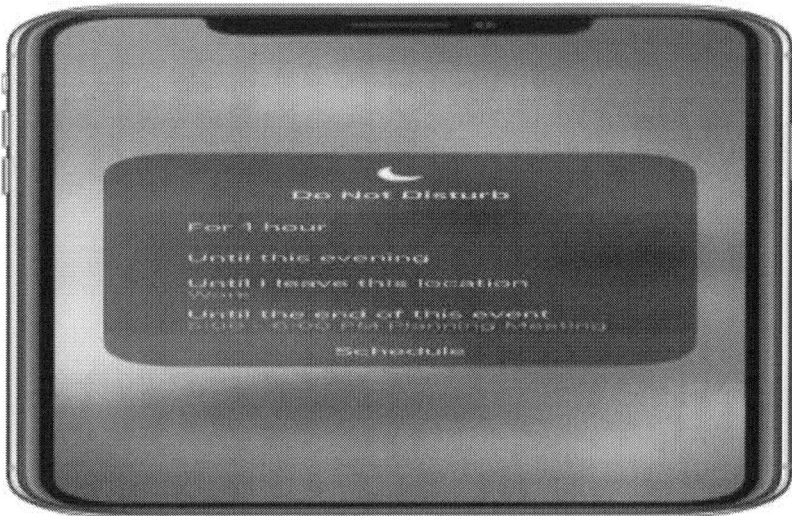

Allow calls when Do Not Disturb is on

1. Open Settings > Do Not Disturb.

2. Do any of the following:

• Tap Allow Calls From: To allow incoming calls from a selected group.

• Turn on Repeated Calls: to allow iPad 8 Gen to receive repeated calls from the same number for emergency purposes.

If Do Not Disturb is turned on, you can still allow calls from emergency contacts

Follow these steps to allow messages and calls from certain contacts, when Do Not Disturb is on:

1. Open the Contacts app.

2. Choose a contact, then tap Edit.

3. Tap Text or Ringtone, then turn on Emergency Bypass.

Or, create a Medical ID, then identify an emergency contact.

Messages and calls will come through from the emergency contacts even if Do Not Disturb is on.

Schedule Quiet Hours

1. Open Settings > Do Not Disturb.

2. Turn on Scheduled, then set a start time and end time for your quiet time.

Choose when Do Not Disturb silences iPad 8 Gen

You can also choose if Do Not Disturb silences iPad 8 Gen only when locked, or when it is also unlocked.

1. Open Settings > Do Not Disturb.

2. Do any of the following:

● Tap always to silence iPad 8 Gen any time Do Not Disturb is on.

● Tap while iPad 8 Gen is unlocked, to silence iPad 8 Gen.

Use Do Not Disturb While Driving, to keep notifications, calls and text messages from distracting you while driving.

You can also turn on Do Not Disturb for bedtime, to dim silence notifications and dim display while sleeping.

Turn on Do Not Disturb While Driving

When you turn on Do Not Disturb While Driving, notifications and text messages will be silenced and limited, allowing you to focus on the road. Ask Siri to read replies to you, so that you won't have to look at your iPad 8 Gen. Incoming calls will only be allowed if you allow them in Do Not Disturb settings.

WARNING: for proper navigation and to avoid distractions. Don't substitute Do Not Disturb While driving, for following the rules that prohibit distracted driving.

Turn on Do Not Disturb While Driving

If your iPad 8 Gen detects that you are driving and you haven't set up Do Not Disturb While Driving, iPad 8 Gen will ask if you want to turn it on. Otherwise, you can activate it manually.

1. Open Settings > Do Not Disturb.

2. Scroll down to find Activate, then tap it.

3. Choose when to turn on Do Not Disturb While Driving.

- Automatically: If your iPad 8 Gen detects you are driving.

- When Connected to Car Bluetooth: If you connect iPad 8 Gen to a car's Bluetooth system.

- Manually: you have to turn it on in Control Center.

• Activate With CarPlay: Automatically activates when your iPad 8 Gen is connected to CarPlay.

If you want to add Do Not Disturb While Driving to Control Center, open Settings > Control Center > Customize Controls, then tap the Insert button near Do Not Disturb While Driving.

Get Calls, Messages, And Notifications When you're A Passenger

Turn off Do Not Disturb While Driving, if it gets activated when you are not driving, such as when you are just a passenger in the car.

1. Tap the Do Not Disturb While Driving notification on your Lock screen.

2. Then, tap I'm Not Driving.

You can swipe up from the bottom of your screen.

Send An Auto-Reply text Message That You're Driving

An auto-reply will be sent to your Favorites group, when Do Not Disturb While Driving is activated by default. Use the following to change who receives the auto-reply.

1. Open Settings > Do Not Disturb > Auto-Reply To.

2. Choose any of the following:

- No One: to turn off auto-reply.

- Recents: to send an auto-reply to anybody, you sent a message in the last two days, even if they're not listed in your Contacts.

- Favorites: To send an auto-reply to anybody in your Favorites group.

- All Contacts: To send an auto-reply to everybody in your Contacts.

If anybody replies your auto-reply with the message "Urgent," every text from that person throughout the remainder of your drive will be allowed through.

Create a Custom Auto Reply Text Message

1. Open Settings, then tap Do Not Disturb > Auto-Reply.

2. Tap a message to bring up the keyboard, then type the new message.

Allow Some Calls

You can allow some calls through, if your car doesn't have Bluetooth or support CarPlay.

• To allow more than one call from the same person within 3 minutes: Open Settings > Do Not Disturb, then turn on Repeated Calls.

• To allow calls from every one or only your Favorites: Open Settings > Do Not Disturb > Allow Calls From.

Note: Do Not Disturb While Driving needs Location Services to determine if you are driving or near your work, home or a predicted destination. If you want to turn off Location Services for Do Not Disturb While Driving, open Settings > Privacy > Location Services > System Services, then turn off Location Based Alerts.

Set Do Not Disturb for bedtime on iPad 8 Gen

To prevent disturbances in your sleep turn on Do Not Disturb. Until you unlock your iPad 8 Gen in the morning, it will silence your calls, dim the display and send overnight notifications to Notification Center.

Turn On Do Not Disturb for Bedtime

1. Open Settings >and select Do Not Disturb.

2. Turn on Do Not Disturb, and then tap to turn on Scheduled.

3. Tap From to set the beginning and ending times for your sleep. Do not Disturb icon display During these hours, in status bar.

4. Turn on Dim Lock Screen.

5. To select **No One** for ignoring incoming calls, tap allow calls.

To ignore incoming calls, tap Allow Calls, and then select **No One**.

Do Not Disturb will automatically turn off at the end of the specified quiet time. To turn it off sooner, tap the Do Not Disturb notification on the Lock screen, and then tap Turn Off. When Do Not Disturb is off, notifications resume.

Chapter 5: Ask Siri on iPad 8 Gen

Talking to Siri is like having a personal assistant that knows your schedule like the back of his hands. A convenient way to handle your schedule, manage your time and be more productive on your device is through Siri. Ask Siri to translate a phrase, set a reminder, send messages to your family and colleagues, find a location, report on the weather, control other applications, and more. The more you use Siri, the better it knows what you need.

To use Siri, iPad 8 Gen must be connected to the Internet, of course, Cellular charges will apply.

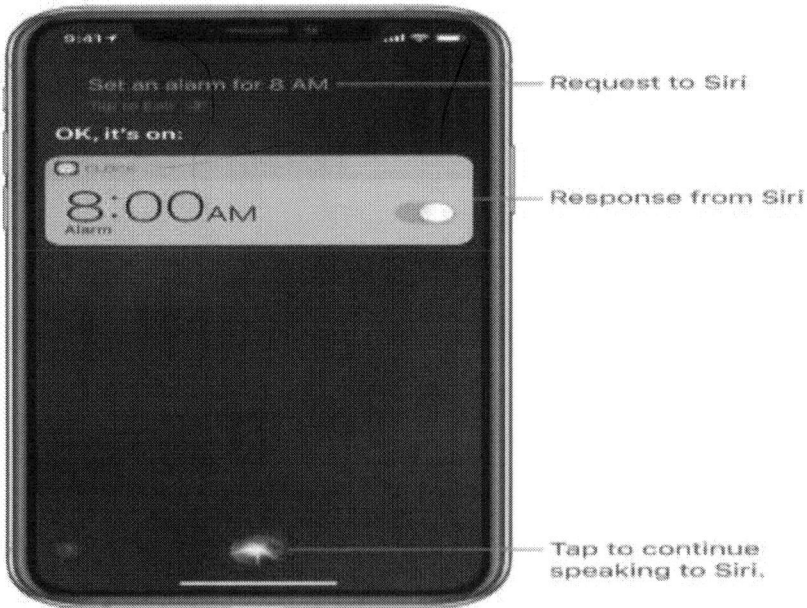

Set up Siri

Create Siri settings on your iPad 8 Gen

1. Click Settings > Siri & Search,
2. Enable the following queries from the options

Listen for "Hey Siri"

Press Side Button for Siri.

Summon Siri with your voice

1. Say "Hey Siri," asking Siri a question or making a request.

For example, say something like "Hey Siri, how's the weather today?" or "Hey Siri, set an alarm for 8 a.m."

2. To ask Siri another question and make subsequent requests, tap the Listen button.

Now this is very important, To prevent iPad 8 Gen from responding to "Hey Siri," place your iPad 8 Gen face down and you can change the settings as well

1. Tap Settings > Siri & Search,
2. Disable Listen for "Hey Siri."

Do one of the following:

Press and hold the side button.

EarPods: Press and hold the center or call button.

AirPods: Double-tap an AirPod. This action can be done simultaneously.

CarPlay: Press and hold the voice command button on the steering wheel, or touch and hold the Home button on the CarPlay infotainment screen.

Siri Eyes Free: Long Press the voice command button on your steering wheel to enable this function.

2. When Siri appears, request an action from Siri or ask a question.

For example, make a request like this from Siri; "What's 18 percent of 225?" or "Set the timer for 3 minutes."

3. Basically, to ask Siri to perform a task, requires that you tap the Listen button. Go ahead and have fun with it.

Make a Correction If Siri Misunderstands You

1. Tap listen button
2. Paraphrase your request to change how you initially structured the instruction.

In order to lay emphasis on your instructions,

1. Click listen button

2. Clearly emphasize the noun or verb in a new request. You can say "Call", entering the name of the person

Adjusting your request with text can be done

1. Click "Tap to Edit" from the dialog box
2. Use the keyboard interface to input instructions

You can also modify a message before it is sent and delivered to the recipient saying "Change it".

Type instead of speaking to Siri

1. Go to Settings

> Accessibility > Siri, , enable Type to Siri.

2. To make a request,   activate Siri, using the keyboard and text field, ask Siri a question.

Your secrets are safe with Siri. It protects your log and does not share it with thirsty third parties leaving you the freedom to choose your shareable content. To learn more,

- Go to Settings > click Siri & Search > tap About Ask Siri & Privacy.

Find out what Siri can do on iPad 8 Gen

Siri is quite fascinating and you might want to try out some activities like searching for information and carrying out duties.

With your voice, Siri begins to handle your requests and command immediately which overlaps into your applications. So basically the function of Siri is to provide special services for you on IPad 8 Gen in comfort.

For example "Hey Siri, set up a meeting with Calvin at 6", Siri goes through your calendar app and reminders and fix an appointment immediately.

Say this the next time you are finding it difficult to translate a language or confused about certain words; "Hey Siri, how do you say thank you in Mandarin? ". Getting information from the web is the sport of Siri and no matter what you are looking for, even silly stuff, it will fish it for you.

Ask Siri these questions " Hey Siri, what causes a rainbow?" "Hey Siri, what is the cosine derivative of x?" From the data provided by Siri, should it involve links to websites, access it with Safari browser and confirm your doubts, except you are not dealing with doubts but hard facts.

In addition, even though Siri is an invisible companion, it wants to interact with you and create a personal relationship. Your requests can fall back as an onscreen dialogue where you take action like clicking some tabs or hitting some keys.

"Hi Siri, play Wild 94.9" or " Hey Siri, tune into ESPN Radio" allows your virtual personal assistant to play your radio stations.

When you want more information about a thing, "Hey Siri, what can you do?" That's some cool stuff! You can use additional assistance by using the Help button while Siri is active.

Tell Siri about yourself on iPad 8 Gen

If you have ever wondered just how Siri make the right guess about you, the name of your sister and your pet, you want to know how this is possible. When Siri knows about you and your residential and workplace address, it gives you personal services. "Call my sister right now", "Send message to my supervisor" are command prompts that will be carried out immediately.

Tell Siri who you are

To have fun with this;

1. Tap contacts
2. Enter your contact details
3. Move to Settings

Tap Siri & Search

- Fill your name in My Information

Ask Siri

You can ditch out Siri command such as "Hey Siri, learn to pronounce my name." You can also tell Siri about a relationship such as "Hey Siri, Eliza Block is my wife" or "Hey Siri, Ashley Kamin is my mom."

How to keep Siri up to date about what it knows about you on Apple devices

To do this, on each device:

1. Go to the Settings.

2. Sign in using the same Apple ID on all your Apple devices.

How to Prevent Siri Information from Getting Updated Across iPad 8 Gen And the Rest of Your Devices

1. Go to Settings.
2. Select [your name].
3. Click on "iCloud."
4. Turn off, Siri.

Note: It is to be noted that Siri makes use of location services when it needs your location to process certain requests. Once you have the Location Services turned on, your device's location at the time a request was made will automatically send to Apple for the response accuracy from Siri to be accurate.

How to Add Siri Shortcuts on iPad 8 Gen

Just as some apps provide shortcuts to gain easy access to things you do on your device frequently, Siri can be asked to help you in getting shortcuts added.

An example is the travel app which helps in displaying your upcoming trip event. With Siri you can just get to ask "Where am I going next?"

• To add a shortcut: If the app offers the shortcuts, select the "Add to Siri" option and follow the onscreen instructions you will be prompted with to get a phrase of your choice recorded which then performs the shortcut.

• Using the shortcut: To do this, call on Siri and speak out your recorded phrase for the shortcut.

• Siri can also help in suggesting shortcuts on the Lock screen when you begin to search depending on your routines and how your apps are put into use.

• If you would like to get the shortcut suggestion for an app turned off, you are required to take the following instructions:

1. Go to Settings

2. Select "Siri & Search."

3. Click on the app.

4. Turn off "Suggest Shortcuts."

About Siri Suggestions on iPad 8 Gen

Siri is designed such that it can make suggestions for what might be in your plan to do next such as confirming an appointment or sending an email depending on your routines and how you make use of your apps.

Siri also helps when you do any of the following:

A glance at the Lock screen or starting a search: Siri can learn your routines which make it easy for it to get a suggestion for what you need at the right time. For instance, if you are a type that is frequently ordering for a coffee mid-morning, Siri will automatically suggest when it's time you normally place your order.

Create email and events: Once you start adding people to an email or calendar event, Siri will learn to automatically suggest the people you must have included in your previous emails or events.

Receive calls: Siri will inform you about the person calling every time you get an incoming call from an unknown number based on the phone numbers that are saved in your emails.

Leave for an event: Siri can review traffic conditions and let you know when to leave if your calendar event includes a location.

See your flight status: Siri can show your flight status in Maps once you have a boarding pass in your Mail or Wallet. Tap the suggestion when you need directions to the airport.

Type: Siri will suggest names of movies, places or anything you have viewed on your iPad 8 Gen recently as you start to type in texts. It also can suggest your estimated time of arrival.

Search in Safari: Siri can suggest your websites and other information while typing in the search field.Siri can suggest words and phrases above the keyboard depending on what you were just reading:

Get appointments confirmed or flight booked on a travel website: Siri will automatically ask if you want to get it added to your calendar.

Read News stories: As Siri begins to learn topics you are interested in, they will get suggested in the News.

To get Siri Suggestions turned off,

1. Go to Settings.

2. Select "Siri & Search."

3. You will then be prompted with the following options, any of which you can turn off;

• Suggestions in Search.

• Suggestions in Lookup.

• Suggestions on Lock Screen.

4. Tap the app and turn off Show Siri Suggestions for a specific app.

Note: It is important to note that personal information which is encrypted and private, stays updated across your devices as long as you are signed in on them using the same Apple ID.

Your Siri experience is improved on your other devices once Siri begins to learn about you on your device.

Siri is designed to help you in protecting your information as well as choosing what to share. To learn more about this, take the following steps:

1. Go to Settings.

2. Select "Siri & Search."

3. Select "About Search Suggestions & Privacy."

Using Siri in Your Car

• Using the CarPlay or Siri Eyes Free, you can concentrate when driving on the road while you make use of Siri to make calls, send text messages, get directions, play songs as well as many other iPad 8 Gen features.

• **CarPlay:** The CarPlay is made available in selected cars taking what you need to do on your iPad 8 Gen and putting them on the built-in display of your car. The CarPlay functions with the use of Siri such that you can ask Siri for what you want.

• **Siri Eyes Free:** Just like the CarPlay, this is also available only in selected cars. It makes use of your voice in getting features of your iPad 8 Gen controlled without having to look or touch your iPad 8 Gen.

• Bluetooth can be used in connecting your iPad 8 Gen to your car. You are advised to refer to your user guide that came with your car if the need arises.

• To summon Siri while in your car, press and hold down the voice command button on your steering wheel until you hear the Siri tone and make your request afterward.

Changing Siri Settings on iPad 8 Gen

The voices for Siri can be altered, prevent intruders from accessing your Siri when your device is locked and many more.

Changing Siri Settings

1. Go to Settings.

2. Select "Siri & Search."

3. Then you can do the following:

● Change the voice for Siri: This setting is not available for all languages. All you need to do is select "Siri Voice" and select a male or female voice for Siri or change the accent.

● Preventing Siri from responding to the voice command "Hey Siri": Turn off Listen for "Hey Sir" option.

● Preventing Siri from responding to the side or Home button: This can be done by turning off Press Side Button for Siri.

● Changing the language Siri responds to: Select Language.

● Limiting when Siri provides voice feedback: If you like to prevent Siri from sending you voice feedback, select the Voice Feedback option and select an option.

● Preventing access to Siri when your iPad 8 Gen is locked: Turn off Allow Siri When Locked option.

Adjusting the Siri voice volume

Make use of the volume buttons to get this done.

Make a Correction If Siri Misunderstands You

- Rephrase your request: Tap the Listen button, then say your request in a different way.

- Spell out part of your request: Tap the Listen button, then repeat your request by spelling out any words that Siri didn't understand. For example, say "Call," then spell the person's name.
- Edit your request with text: Above the response from Siri, tap "Tap to Edit," then use the onscreen keyboard.
- Change a message before sending it: Say "Change it."

Type Instead of Speaking to Siri

1. Go to Settings > Accessibility > Siri, then turn on Type to Siri.

2. To make a request, summon Siri, then use the keyboard and text field to ask Siri a question or to do a task for you.

Siri is designed to protect your information, and you can choose what you share. To learn more, go to Settings > Siri & Search > About Ask Siri & Privacy.

Send Animated Animoji or Memoji Recordings

You can send Animoji and Memoji messages that use your voice and mirror your facial expressions.

1. In a conversation, tap the Animoji button, then choose an Animoji or Memoji.

2. Tap the Record button to record your facial expressions and voice. Tap the red square to stop recording.

Tap Replay to review your message.

3. Tap the Send button to send your message or the Delete button to cancel.

You can also take a picture or video of yourself as an Animoji or Memoji, decorate it with stickers, then send it. Or you can become an Animoji or Memoji in a FaceTime conversation.

Edit your Messages name and photo

In Messages you can share your name and photo with contacts when you start or respond to a new Message conversation. You can use an Animoji, Memoji, or custom image for your photo.

Open Messages, tap the More Options button, tap Edit Name and Photo, then do any of the following:

- Change your profile image: Tap Edit, then choose an option.
- Change your name: Tap the text fields where your name appears.
- Turn sharing on or off: Tap the button next to Name and Photo Sharing (green indicates that it's on).

- Change who can see your profile: Tap an option below Share Automatically (Name and Photo Sharing must be turned on).

You can also use the name and photo in your Messages profile for your Apple ID and Contacts name and photo.

Switch from a Message conversation to a FaceTime call

In a Message conversation, you can initiate a FaceTime call with the person you're chatting with in Messages.

1. In a Message conversation, tap the profile picture or the name at the top of the conversation.

2. Tap FaceTime.

Use Business Chat

(U.S. only; beta) In Messages, you can communicate with businesses that offer Business Chat. You can get answers to questions, resolve issues, get advice on what to buy, make purchases with Apple Pay, and more.

1. Search for the business you want to chat with using Maps, Safari, Search, or Siri.

2. Start a conversation by tapping a chat link in the search results—for example, the blue Business chat button, the company logo, or a text link (the appearance of the chat link varies with the context).

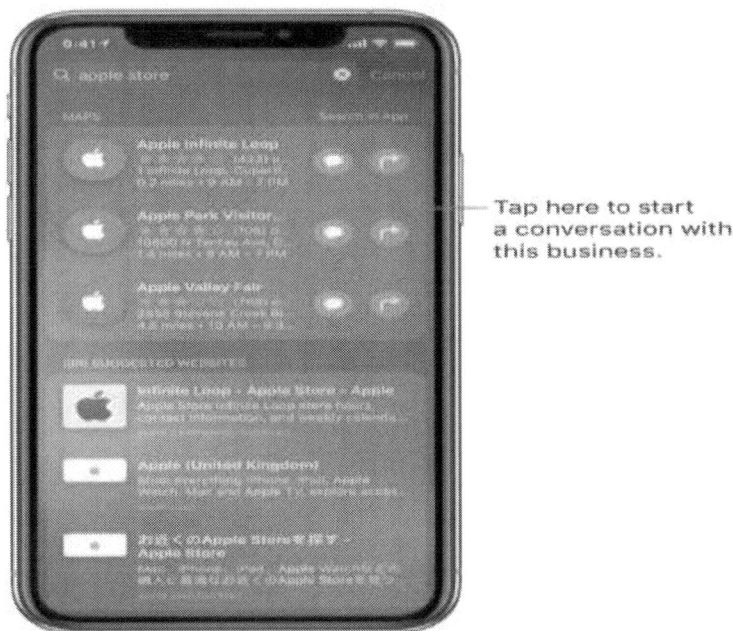

Tap here to start a conversation with this business.

You can also initiate a chat with some businesses from their website or iOS app.

Note: Business Chat messages you send appear in dark gray, to distinguish them from iMessages (blue) and SMS/MMS messages (green).

Type and edit text on iPad 8 Gen

You can use the onscreen keyboard to add and edit text in iPad 8 Gen apps.

Enter Text Using the Onscreen Keyboard

In any app that allows text editing, open the onscreen keyboard by tapping a text field. Tap individual keys to type, or use QuickPath (not available for all languages) to type a word by sliding from one letter to the next without lifting your finger. To end the word, lift your finger.

You can use either method as you type, and even switch in the middle of a sentence. (If you tap the Delete key after sliding to type a word, it deletes the whole word.)

Note: As you slide to type, you see suggested alternatives to the word you're entering, rather than predictions for your next word.

While entering text, you can do any of the following:

- Type uppercase letters: Tap Shift, or touch the Shift key and slide to a letter.
- Turn on Caps Lock: Double-tap Shift.
- Quickly end a sentence with a period and a space: Double-tap the Spacebar.
- Enter numbers, punctuation, or symbols: Tap the Number key or the Symbol key .
- Undo the last edit: Swipe left with three fingers.
- Redo the last edit: Swipe right with three fingers.
- Enter emoji: Tap the Next Keyboard, Emoji button or the Next Keyboard button to switch to the Emoji keyboard.
- Enter accented letters or other alternate characters: Touch and hold a key, then slide to choose one of the options.

You can also dictate text or use Magic Keyboard (available separately) to enter text.

Set Typing Options

You can turn typing features, such as spell check and auto-correction, on or off.

1. While typing text using the onscreen keyboard, touch and hold the Next Keyboard Emoji key or the Switch Keyboard key, then slide to Keyboard Settings. You can also go to Settings > General > Keyboard.

2. In the list, turn special typing features on or off.

Turn your keyboard into a trackpad

1. Touch and hold the Spacebar with one finger until the keyboard turns light gray.

2. Move the insertion point by dragging around the keyboard.

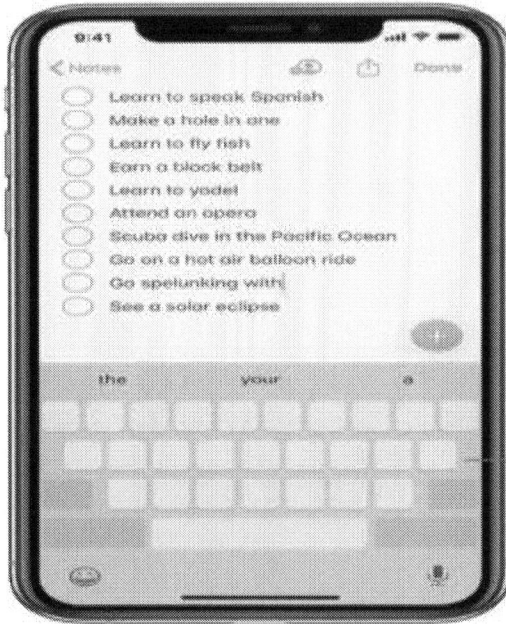

Drag around the keyboard to move the insertion point.

How to use Memoji in Messages on iPad

Just like a combination of meme and emoji. You can now select from over 15 faces, age and hair options to reflect different personality and profession.

How to create your own Memoji

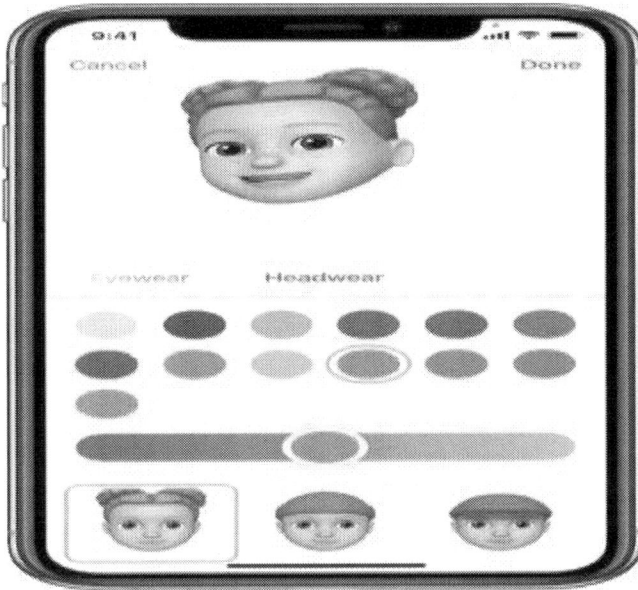

1. Tap the Memoji Stickers button in any conversation of your choice, then touch the New Memoji button.

2. Customize as you which by choosing from the available features.

3. Tap Done to add the Memoji..

You can also edit, duplicate, or delete a Memoji by just tapping the Memoji Stickers button, touch the concerned Memoji , then click the More Options button.

How to send Memoji and Memoji stickers

1. Touch Memoji Stickers button.

2. To view the stickers in the sticker pack, tap a memoji in the top row.

3. To send a sticker,

  - Tap the desired sticker to add it to the message and tap the Send button or

Touch and hold the sticker, drag to top of a message in the conversation. The sticker is then sent automatically.

To send animated Memoji or Memoji recordings,

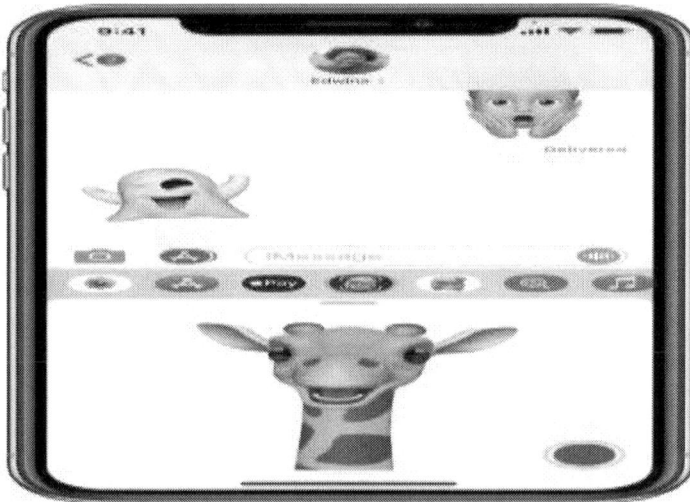

1. Tap the Memoji button in any conversation of your choice, then choose any Memoji.

2. Record your facial expressions or voice by tapping the record button. When you're done, touch the red button. If you wish to review your message, tap replay.

3. Tap the Send or delete button as you desire.

Share Audio with Airpods And beats Headphones From IPad 8 Gen

While you wear AirPods or compatible Beats headphones or earphones, you can share what you're listening to with a friend who's also wearing AirPods or compatible Beats headphones or earphones.

Both sets of audio devices must be paired with iPad 8 Gen, iPhone, or iPod touch.

Start sharing when your friend's earphones are in the charging case

Your earphones or headphones should be connected to your iPad 8 Gen, and your friend's earphones should be inside their case and connected to your friend's iPad 8 Gen, iPhone, or iPod touch.

1. While you're wearing your earphones or headphones, move your iPad 8 Gen close to your friend's open charging case.

2. On your iPad 8 Gen, tap Temporarily Share Audio, then follow the onscreen instructions.

To ensure an earphone or headphone set is connected, go to Settings > Bluetooth. To connect a set, tap its name under My Devices.

Start sharing with your friend's Beats Studio3 Wireless or Beats Solo3 Wireless headphones

1. Ask your friend to briefly press (for less than 1 second) the power button on their headphones.

2. While you're wearing your earphones or headphones, move your iPad 8 Gen close to your friend's headphones.

3. On your iPad 8 Gen, tap Temporarily Share Audio, then follow the onscreen instructions.

Start sharing when your friend is wearing earphones or headphones

If your friend is wearing earphones or headphones connected to their iPad 8 Gen, iPhone, or iPod touch, you can share the audio that's playing on your iPad 8 Gen.

1. Wear your earphones or headphones.

2. On your iPad 8 Gen, tap the Playback Destination button in the Now Playing controls, either in the app you're listening to or on the Lock screen.

Or open Control Center, touch and hold the Now Playing controls at the top right, then tap the Playback Destination button.

3. Tap Share Audio (below the name of your earphones or headphones).

4. Bring your iPad 8 Gen close to your friend's iPad 8 Gen, iPhone, or iPod touch.

5. Tap Share Audio on your iPad 8 Gen.

6. Ask your friend to tap Join on their device.

Separately control the volume of each set of earphones or headphones

1. On your iPad 8 Gen, open Control Center, then touch and hold the volume control.

2. Drag the separate volume sliders.

Stop Sharing Audio

On your iPad 8 Gen, tap the Playback Destination button in the Now Playing controls, then tap the name of your friend's earphones or headphones to turn off the connection.

Or open Control Center, touch and hold the Now Playing controls at the top right, tap the Playback Destination button, then tap the name of your friend's earphones or headphones.

View health and fitness information on iPad 8 Gen

In the Health app , find health and fitness information about yourself in one place.

View your highlights

Tap Summary at the lower left, then scroll down to see highlights of your recent health and fitness data.

To see more details about a category, tap the Details button.

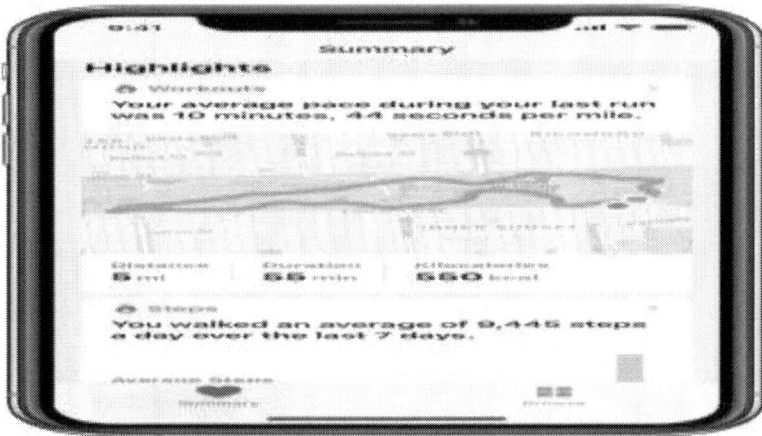

Add or remove a health category from Favorites on the Summary screen

Tap Summary at the lower left, tap Edit for the Favorites section, tap a category to turn it on or off, then tap Done.

View details in the health categories

Tap Browse at the bottom right to display the Health Categories screen, then do one of the following:

- Tap a category. (To see all categories, scroll up and down.)

- Tap the search field, then type the name of a category (such as Nutrition) or a specific type of data (such as Protein).

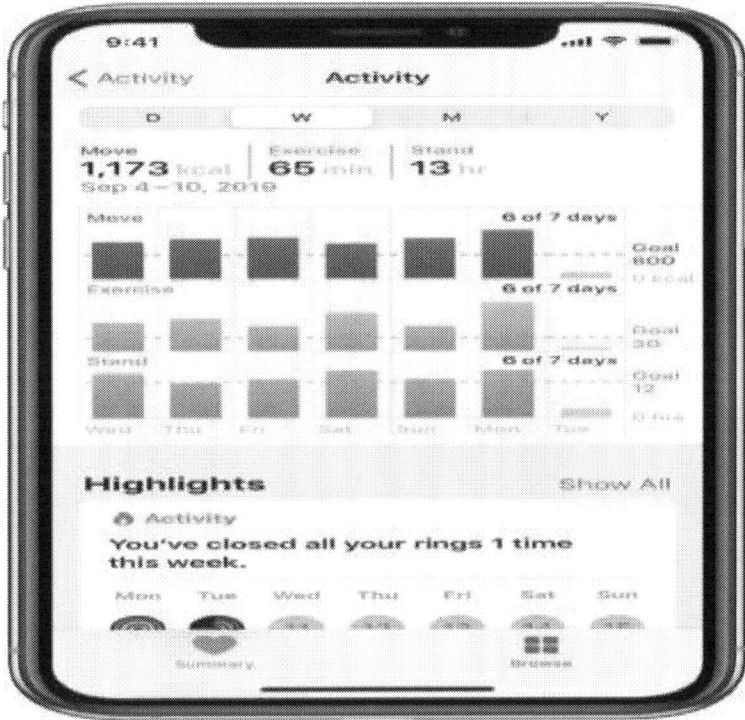

To view details about any of the data, tap the Details button. Depending on the data type, you may be able to do the following:

- See weekly, monthly, and yearly views of the data: Tap the tabs at the top of the screen.
- Manually enter data: Tap Add Data in the top-right corner of the screen.

- Move a data type to Favorites on the Summary screen: Turn on Add to Favorites. (Scroll down if you don't see Add to Favorites.)

- View which apps and devices are allowed to share data: Tap Data Sources & Access below Options. (Scroll down if you don't see Options.)

- Delete data: Tap Show All Data below Options, swipe left on a data record, then tap Delete. To delete all data, tap Edit, then tap Delete All.

- Change the measurement unit: Tap Unit below Options, then select a different unit.

Learn More about Health and Fitness

The bottom of the Summary screen provides introductory articles, app suggestions, and other information. Tap an item to learn more.

When you view health category details, many categories also show recommended apps.

Track your menstrual cycle on iPad 8 Gen

In the Health app , track your menstrual cycle to get period and fertility window predictions.

Get started with cycle tracking

1. Tap Browse at the bottom right, then tap Cycle Tracking.

2. Tap Get Started, then follow the onscreen instructions.

To help improve predictions for your period and fertility window, enter the requested information about your last period.

Log Your Cycle Information

1. Tap Browse at the bottom right, then tap Cycle Tracking.

2. Do any of the following:

- Log a period day: Tap a day in the timeline at the top of the screen. To log the flow level for that day, tap Period below Cycle Log, then choose an option.

Or tap Add Period at the top right, then select days from the monthly calendar.

Logged days are marked on the timeline with solid red circles. To remove a logged day, tap it.

- Log symptoms: Drag the timeline at the top of the screen to select a day, tap Symptoms, then select all that apply. When finished, tap Done. Days with symptoms are represented by purple dots.

- Log spotting: Drag the timeline to select a day, tap Spotting, choose Had Spotting, then tap Done.

3. To add additional categories, such as ovulation test results and basal body temperature, tap Options, then choose the categories.

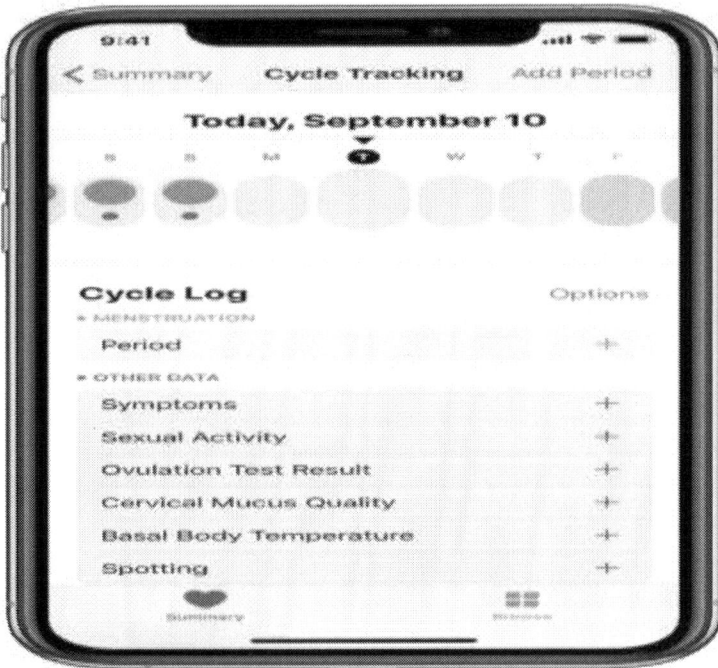

View the cycle timeline

Tap Browse at the bottom right, then tap Cycle Tracking. Timeline information is displayed in the following format:

- Solid red circles: Days you logged for your period.

- Purple dots: Days you logged for having symptoms.

- Light red circles: Your period prediction.

To hide or show predicted period days, tap Options, then turn Period Prediction off or on.

- Light blue days: A prediction of your likely fertility window. Fertility window predictions should not be used as a form of birth control.

To show or hide the fertile window prediction, tap Options, then turn Fertility Prediction on or off.

To select different days, drag the timeline. Data that you logged for the selected day appears below in the Cycle Log.

Change Period and Fertility Notifications and Other Cycle Tracking Options

1. Tap Browse at the bottom right, then tap Cycle Tracking.

2. Scroll down, then tap Options.

3. To turn an option on or off, tap it.

View Your Cycle History and Statistics

1. Tap Browse at the bottom right, then tap Cycle Tracking.

2. Scroll down to see timelines of your three most recent periods; scroll further to see related statistics.

3. To see more details and older information for Cycle History or Statistics, tap the Details button in that portion of the screen.

To find only the days that match a particular symptom or flow level in the detailed Cycle History, tap Filters at the top right, choose an option, then tap Done.

Set reminders on iPad 8 Gen

In the Reminders app , you can easily create and organize reminders to keep track of all of life's to-dos. Use it for shopping lists, projects at work, tasks around the house, and anything else you want to track. Create subtasks, set flags, add attachments, and choose when and where to receive reminders. You can also use smart lists to automatically organize your reminders.

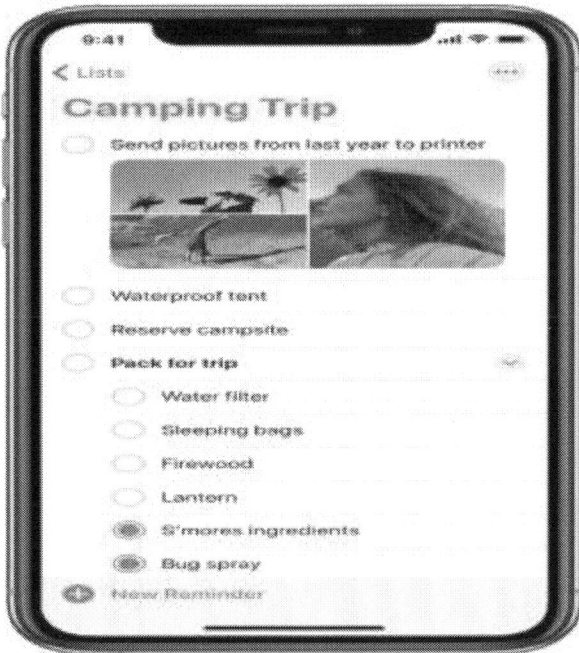

Keep Your Reminders up To date on All Your Devices with Icloud

Go to Settings > [your name] > iCloud, then turn on Reminders.

Your iCloud reminders—and any changes you make to them—appear on your iPad 8 Gen, iPad 8 Gen, iPod touch, Apple Watch, and Mac where you're signed in with your Apple ID.

Note: If you've been using an earlier version of Reminders, you may need to upgrade your iCloud reminders to use features such as attachments, flags, subtasks, grouped lists, list colors and icons, and more. To upgrade, tap the Upgrade button next to your iCloud account in Reminders. (You may need to tap Lists at the top left to see your iCloud account.)

Also note the following:

- Upgraded reminders are not backward compatible with the Reminders app in earlier versions of iOS and macOS.

- Until macOS Catalina is available, your Mac using the same iCloud account can't access your upgraded reminders.

Add a reminder

Ask Siri. Say something like: "Add artichokes to my groceries list.

Or do the following in a list:

1. Tap New Reminder, then enter text.

2. Use the quick toolbar above the keyboard to do any of the following:

- Schedule a date or time: Tap the Time button, then choose a date for an all-day reminder or tap Custom to set a date and time for the notification.
- Add a location: Tap the Location button, then choose where you want to be reminded—for example, when you leave work or arrive at home.
- Set a flag: Tap the Flag button to mark an important reminder.
- Attach a photo or scanned document: Tap the Photos button, then take a new photo, choose an existing photo from your photo library, or scan a document.

3. To add more details to the reminder, tap the Edit Details button, then do any of the following:

- Add notes: In the Notes field, enter more info about the reminder.
- Add a web link: In the URL field, enter a web address. Reminders displays the link as a thumbnail that you can tap to go to the website.
- Get a reminder when chatting with someone in Messages: Turn on "Remind me when messaging," then choose someone from your contacts list. The reminder appears the next time you chat with that person in Messages.
- Set a priority: Tap Priority, then choose an option.

4. Tap Done.

Tip: With OS X 10.10 or later, you can hand off reminders you're editing between your Mac and iPad 8 Gen.

Mark A Reminder as Complete

Tap the empty circle next to the reminder.

Completed reminders are hidden the next time you view the list. To unhide completed reminders, tap the More button, then tap Show Completed.

Move or delete reminders

- Reorder reminders in a list: Touch and hold a reminder you want to move, then drag it to a new location.

- Make a subtask: Swipe right on the reminder, then tap Indent. Or drag a reminder onto another reminder.

If you delete or move a parent task, subtasks are also deleted or moved. If you complete a parent task, subtasks are also completed.

- Move a reminder to a different list: Tap the reminder, tap the Edit Details button, tap List, then choose a list.
- Delete a reminder: Swipe left on the reminder, then tap Delete.

To recover a deleted reminder, shake to undo or swipe left with three fingers.

Change your Reminders settings

1. Go to Settings > Reminders.

2. Choose options such as the following:

- Default List: Choose the list for new reminders you create outside of a specific list, such as reminders you create using Siri.

- Today Notification: Set a time to show notifications in Today View for all-day reminders that have been assigned a date without a time.

- Show Reminders as Overdue: The scheduled date turns red for overdue all-day reminders.

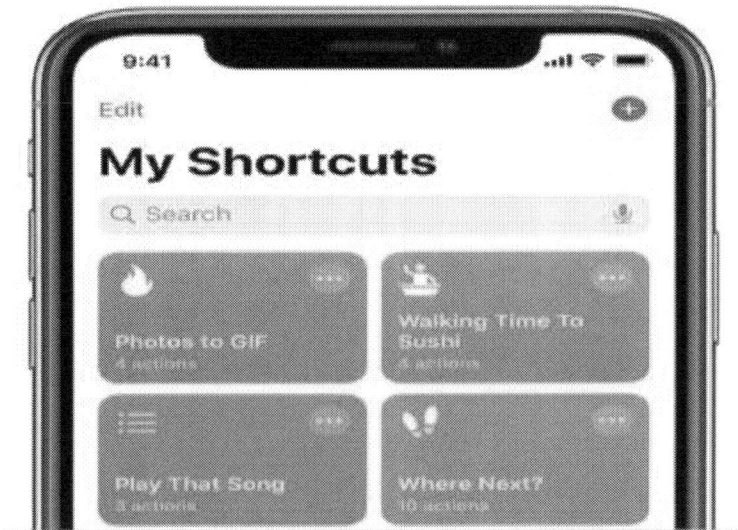

What's A Shortcut?

A shortcut is a quick way to get one or more tasks done with your apps. The Shortcuts app lets you create your own shortcuts with multiple steps. For example, build a "Surf Time" shortcut that grabs the surf report, gives an ETA to the beach, and launches your surf music playlist.

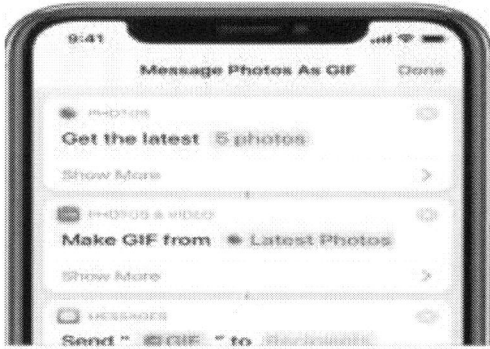

What's an action?

An action—the building block of a shortcut—is a single step in a task. Mix and match actions to create shortcuts that interact with the apps and content on your iOS or iPad 8 GenOS device, as well as with content and services on the Internet. Each shortcut is made up of one or more actions.

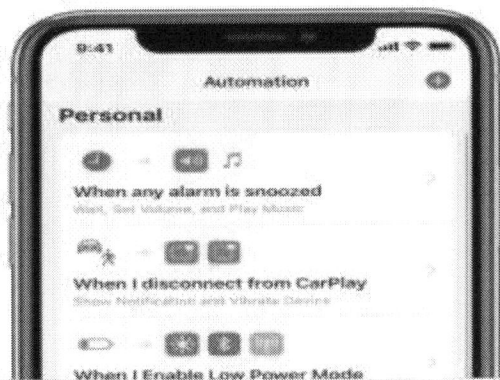

What is automation?

Automation is a type of shortcut that's triggered by an event, rather than manually. You can use the Shortcuts app to set up a personal or home automation and then have the automated shortcut triggered by your arrival, your departure, a setting on your iPad 8 Gen, a time of day, and much more.

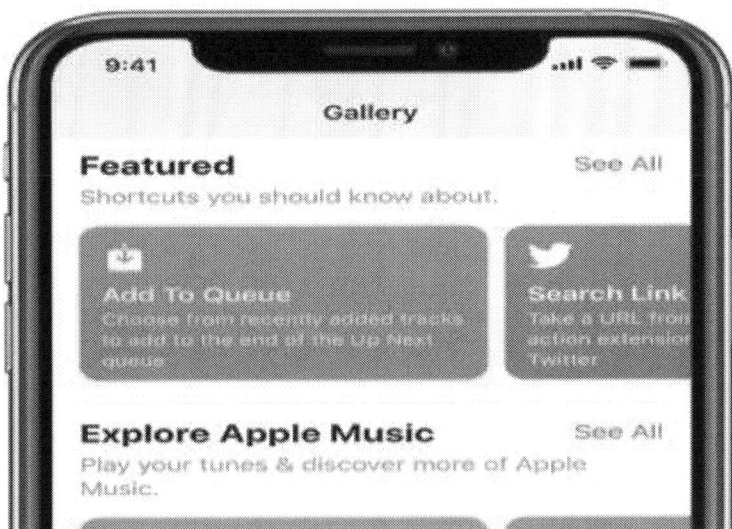

Where do I find shortcuts?

The Gallery features a curated collection of creative and useful shortcuts. Explore the Gallery to check out shortcut possibilities and to see how they're built. When you find a Gallery shortcut you like, add it to your My Shortcuts collection with a simple tap and customize it to suit your needs.

Intro to CarPlay and iPad 8 Gen

Connect your iPad 8 Gen to CarPlay to get turn-by-turn directions, make phone calls, listen to music, check your calendar, and more—all from your car's display.

Note: CarPlay is available only in certain regions (see the iOS Feature Availability website).

CarPlay is available on selected automobiles and on selected aftermarket navigation systems.

Set which apps can access your location on iPad 8 Gen

With Location Services, you can choose which location-based apps—for example, Reminders, Maps, Camera, and Wallet—can gather and use data indicating your location.

Your approximate location is determined using information about your cellular network, local Wi-Fi networks (if you have Wi-

Fi turned on), and GPS (if available). When an app is using Location Services, the Location Services icon appears in the status bar.

Turn on Location Services

If you didn't turn on Location Services when you first set up iPad 8 Gen, go to Settings > Privacy > Location Services, then turn on Location Services.

Turn off Location Services

Go to Settings > Privacy > Location Services,   then choose from the options to turn off Location Services for some apps and services, or for all of them.

If you turn off Location Services, you're asked to turn it on again the next time an app or service tries to use it.

Review the terms and privacy policy for each third-party app to understand how it uses the data it's requesting.

Hide the Map In location Services Alerts

When you allow an app to always use your location in the background, you may receive alerts about the app's use of that information. (These alerts let you change your permission, if you want to.) In the alerts, a map shows locations recently accessed by the app.

To hide the map, go to Settings > Privacy > Location Services >
Location Alerts, then turn off Show Map in
Location Alerts.

With the setting off, you continue to receive location alerts, but
the map isn't shown.

Change   Location   Services settings   for   System Services

Several system services, such as location-based suggestions and
location-based ads, use Location Services.

To see the status for each service, to turn Location Services on or
off for each service, or to show the Location Services icon in the
status bar when enabled system services use your location, go to
Settings > Privacy > Location Services > System Services.

Delete Significant Locations

The Maps app keeps track of the places you've recently visited, as
well as when and how often you visit them. Maps uses this
information to provide you with personalized services like
predictive traffic routing. You can delete this information.

1. Go to Settings > Privacy > Location Services > System Services >
Significant Locations.

2. Do one of the following:

• Delete a single location: Tap the location, tap Edit, then tap the Delete button.

• Delete all locations: Tap Clear History. This action clears all your significant locations on any devices that are signed in with the same Apple ID.

Optimize iPad 8 Gen battery charging

iPad 8 Gen has a setting that helps slow the rate of your battery's aging by reducing the time it spends fully charged. This setting uses machine learning to understand your daily charging routine, then waits to finish charging past 80% until you need it.

1. Go to Settings > Battery, then tap Battery Health.

2. Turn on Optimized Battery Charging.

Get Tips on IPad 8 Gen

In the Tips app , see collections of tips that help you get the most from iPad 8 Gen.

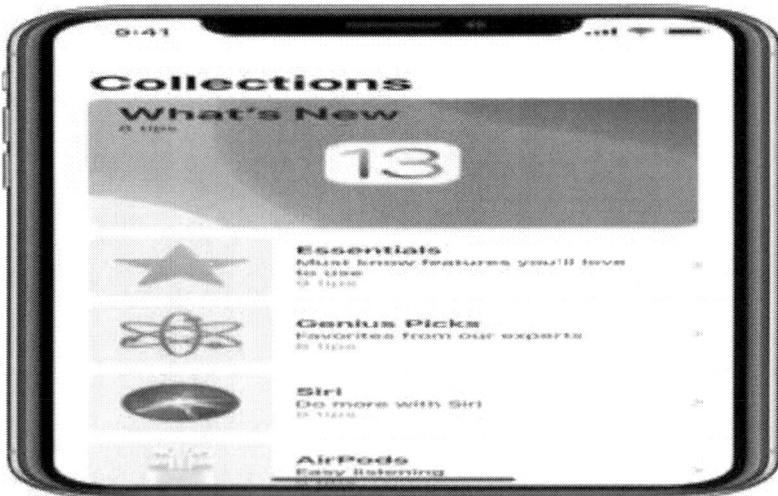

Get Tips

In the Tips app, tap a collection to learn how to take better photos, use dictation, create a custom radio station, and much more. New tips are added frequently.

Get Notified When New Tips Arrive

1. Go to Settings , then tap Notifications.

2. Tap Tips below Notification Style, then turn on Allow Notifications.

3. Choose options for the location and style of tip notifications, when they should appear, and so on.

Allow Others to Control Accessories in Your Home

In the Home app , you can invite other people to control your smart accessories. You and the people you invite need to be signed in to iCloud and have iPad 8 GenOS 13. You also need to be at your home or have a home hub set up in your home.

I

nvite Others to Control Accessories

1. Tap the Home tab, then tap the Add and Edit Home button in the top-left corner of the screen.

2. Tap Invite.

If you set up more than one home, tap Home Settings, then tap a home.

3. Tap the Add button to choose people with an Apple ID from your contacts list, or enter their Apple ID email addresses in the To field.

4. Tap Send Invite.

5. Ask the invitee to do one of the following:

- In the notification: (iOS or iPad 8 GenOS device) Tap Accept.
- In the Home app: (iOS or iPad 8 GenOS device) Tap the Add and Edit Home button, then tap their name.

- On Apple TV: Tap Show Me on Apple TV, then turn on one or more Apple TsVs.

Allow others to access your AirPlay 2-enabled speakers and TVs

1. Tap the Home tab, then tap the Add and Edit Home button.

2. Tap Allow Speaker & TV Access, then choose an option.

You can allow everyone, anyone on the same network, or only people you've invited to share the home. You can also require a password that allows speaker access.

Get music, movies, TV shows, and more in the iTunes Store on iPad 8 Gen

Use the iTunes Store app to add music, movies, and TV shows to iPad 8 Gen.

Find music, movies, TV shows, and more

1. In the iTunes Store, tap any of the following:

- Music, Movies, or TV Shows: Browse by category. To refine your browsing, tap Genres at the top of the screen.
- Charts: See what's popular on iTunes.

- Search: Enter what you're looking for, then tap Search on the keyboard.
- More: Browse Genius recommendations or Tones.

2. Tap an item to see more information about it. You can preview songs, watch trailers for movies and TV shows, or tap the Share button to do any of the following:

- Share a link to the item: Chooses a sharing option.
- Give the item as a gift: Tap Gift.
- Add the item to your wish list: Tap Add to Wish List.

To view your wish list, tap the Item List button, then tap Wish List.

Buy and Download Content

1. To buy an item, tap the price. If the item is free, tap Get.

If you see the Download button instead of a price, you already purchased the item, and you can download it again without a charge.

2. If required, authenticate your Apple ID with Face ID, Touch ID, or your passcode to complete the purchase.

3. To see the progress of a download, tap More, then tap Downloads.

Write an email in Mail on iPad 8 Gen

With the Mail app , you can write and edit emails, and send and receive photos, videos, drawings,   documents, and more.

Create An Email Message

Ask Siri. Say something like: "New email to John Bishop" or "Email Simon and say I got the forms, thanks."

Or do the following:

1. Tap the Compose button.

2. Tap in the email, then type your message.

With the onscreen keyboard, you can tap individual keys or slide your finger from one letter to the next to type without lifting your finger.

3. To change the formatting, tap the Expand Toolbar button in the format bar above the keyboard, then tap the Text Styles button.

You can change the font style, change the color of text, use a bold or italic stye, add a bulleted or numbered list, and more.

Reply to An Email

1. Tap in the email, tap the Reply button, then tap Reply.

2. Type your response.

With the onscreen keyboard, you can tap individual keys or slide your finger from one letter to the next to type without lifting your finger.

Quote some text when you reply to an email

When you reply to an email, you can include text from the sender to clarify what you're responding to.

1. In the sender's email, touch and hold the first word of the text, then drag to the last word.

2. Tap the Reply button, tap Reply, then type your message.

To turn off the indentation of quoted text, go to Settings > Mail > Increase Quote Level.

Add attachments to an email on iPad 8 Gen

In the Mail app , you can attach photos, videos, scanned documents, and more to an email.

Attach a Document To An Email

You can attach a saved document to an email.

1. Tap in the email where you want to insert the document, then tap the Expand Toolbar button in the format bar above the keyboard.

2. Tap the Insert Attachment button above the keyboard, then locate the document in Files.

In Files, tap Browse or Recent at the bottom of the screen, then tap a file, location, or folder to open it.

3. Tap the document to insert it into your email.

You can also use drag and drop to attach a file to your email.

Insert a Saved photo or Video

1. Tap in the email where you want to insert the photo or video, then tap the Expand Toolbar button in the format bar above the keyboard.

2. Tap the Insert Photo Toolbar button in the format bar, then locate the photo or video in the photo selector.

You can swipe up to see more images.

3. Tap the photo or video to insert it into your email.

Take A Photo Or Video To Insert Into An Email

1. Tap in the email where you want to insert the photo or video, then tap the Expand Toolbar button above the keyboard.

2. Tap the Take Photo or Video Toolbar button above the keyboard, then take a new photo or video.

3. Tap Use Photo or Use Video to insert it into your email, or tap Retake if you want to reshoot it.

Scan a document into an email

1. Tap in the email where you want to insert the scanned document, then tap the Expand Toolbar button above the keyboard.

2. Tap the Scan Document Toolbar button above the keyboard.

3. Position iPad 8 Gen so that the document page appears on the screen—iPad 8 Gen automatically captures the page.

To capture the page manually, tap the Take Picture button or press a volume button. To turn the flash on or off, tap the Show Flash Settings button.

4. Scan additional pages, then tap Save when you're done.

5. To make changes to the saved scan, tap it, then do any of the following:

- Crop the image: Tap the Crop button.
- Apply a filter: Tap the Show Filter Settings button.
- Rotate the image: Tap the Rotate button.
- Delete the scan: Tap the Delete scan button.

Mark up an attachment

You can use Markup to write or draw on a photo, video, or PDF attachment.

1. In the email, tap the attachment, then tap the Markup button.

2. Using the drawing tools, draw with your finger.

3. When you're finished, tap Done.

105

Tap to add text, signatures, or shapes, or use the Magnifier.

Tap to choose a color.

Select a drawing tool, the eraser, or the selection tool.

Draw in Your Email

1. Tap in the email where you want to insert a drawing, then tap the Expand Toolbar button above the keyboard.

2. Tap the Markup button in the format bar.

3. Choose a drawing tool and color, then write or draw with your finger.

4. When you're finished, tap Done, then tap Insert Drawing.

To resume work on a drawing, tap the drawing, then tap the Markup button.

Chapter 6: Type and Edit Text on iPad 8 Gen

You can use the onscreen keyboard to add and edit text in iPad 8 Gen apps.

Enter Text Using the Onscreen Keyboard

In any app that allows text editing, you can open the onscreen keyboard by tapping a text field. Also, you can type by tapping keys, or use QuickPath to type a word by sliding from one letter to the next without lifting your finger.

And lift your finger to end the word. Also you can use either method as you type, and even switch in the middle of a sentence. (you can also tap the Delete key⊗ after sliding to type a word, it deletes the whole word at once.)

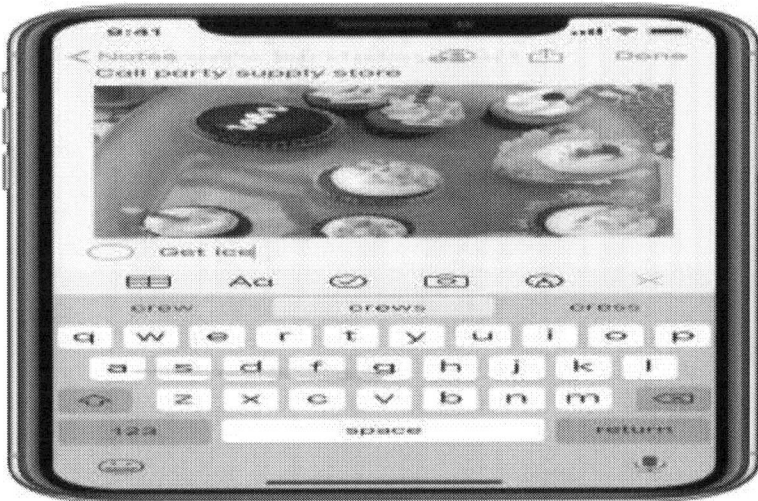

Note: As you slide to type word, Siri suggests alternatives to the word you're entering, rather than predictions for your next word. While typing text, you can do any of the following:

- Type uppercase letters: or Tap Shift, or touch the Shift key and slide to a letter.
- Double-tap Shift to turn on Caps Lock
- Double-tap the Spacebar to Quickly end a sentence with a period and a space
- Tap the Number key .?123 or the Symbol key #+= to Entering numbers, punctuation, or symbols:
- Swipe left with three fingers to Undo the last edit **or tap** ↶ or ↰
- Swipe right with three fingers to Redo the last edit or tap ↷.
- To switch on Emoji Keyboard:

Tap the Next Keyboard button ⊕ or Emoji button ☺.

- To enter accented letters or any alternate: Touch and hold a key, then slide to choose one of the options.

To hide the onscreen keyboard, tap the keyboard key ⌨ .

You can also use Magic Keyboard or dictate text (available separately).

Correct Spelling

You can correct incorrectly spelled words that are underlined in red

1. Tap the underlined word to show suggested corrections.

2. Tap a suggestion to correct the underlined word.

Type the correction If the word you want doesn't appear

Type with One Hand

You can move the keys closer to your thumb to make it easier to type with your one.

1. To switch on keyboard key, touch and hold the Next keyboard Emoji.

2. To choose one of the keyboard layouts (For example, to choose the Right-Handed Layout move the keyboard to the right side of the screen.)

And to let the keyboard at the centre again, tap the right or left edge of the keyboard.

Set Typing Options

You can turn on or off typing features, such as spell check and auto-correction.

1. While typing text,using the onscreen keyboard, you can touch and hold the Next Keyboard Emoji ☺ key or the Switch Keyboard key ⊕and then slide to Keyboard Settings or you can go to Settings > General > Keyboard.

2. Turn special typing features on or off In the list.

Select and Revise Text

To select insert, revise, or replace text, do any of the following:

• To Navigate a long document: Touch and hold the right edge of the document, then drag the scrollbar to locate the text you want to revise.

• To Insert text: Tap to place the insertion point where you want to insert the text or you can also move the insertion point precisely by dragging it and then start typing.

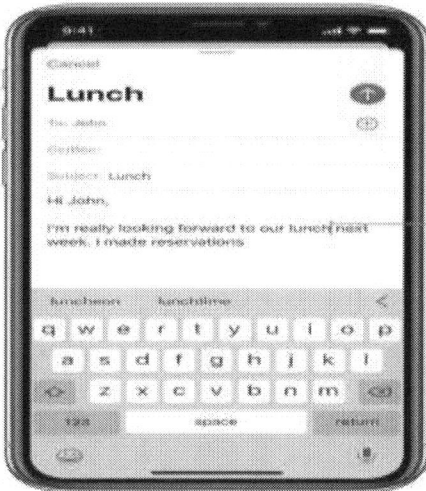

Tap to place the insertion point, or move the insertion point by dragging it.

- To select a word: Double-tap the word with one finger.

- To select a sentence: Triple-tap the sentence with one finger.

- To select a paragraph: Quadruple-tap with one finger.

- To select a block of text: Touch and hold the first word in the block then drag to the last word.

Tap the selection to see options after selecting the text you want to revise or type.

To Cut: Tap Cut or pinch closed with three fingers two times.

To Copy: Tap Copy or pinch closed with three fingers.

To Paste: Tap Paste or pinch open with three fingers.

To Replace: View suggested replacement text, or let Siri suggest alternative text.

- To select B/I/U: Format the selected text.

- To Show More button: View more options.

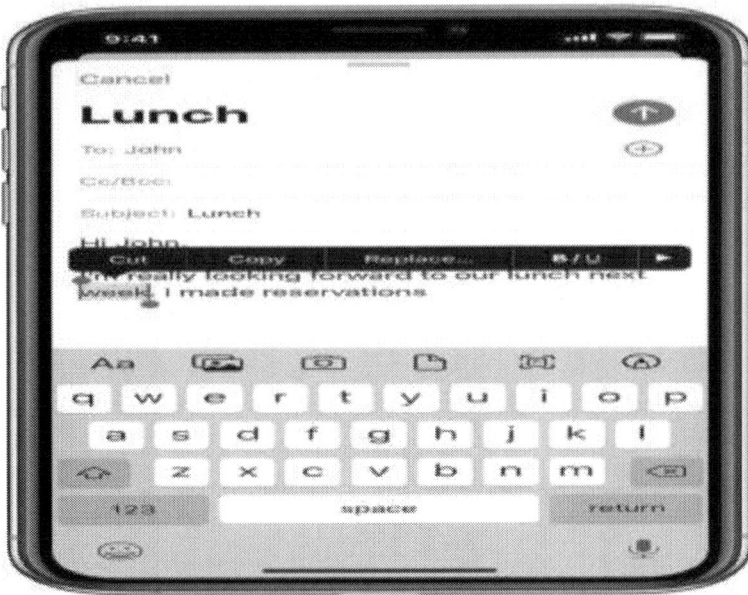

On Universal Clipboard, you can cut or copy something on one Apple device and paste it to another or use drag and drop to move selected text within an app.

Turn Your Keyboard into a Trackpad

1. Use one finger to touch and hold the space bar until the keyboard turn to light gray.

2. Drag around the keyboard to move the insertion point.

Use Predictive Text on IPad 8 Gen

While typing text on the iPad 8 Gen keyboard, Siri can predicts the next word, suggests emoji that could take the place of the word, and also makes other suggestions based on the recent activity and information from the apps (not available for all languages).

For example, type any of these in Messages:

• "I'm at" followed by a space, then your current location will be displayed.

• "My number is" followed by a space, then your phone number will be displayed.

Accept Or Reject A predictive Text Suggestion

Do any of the following while typing text:

To accept a suggested word or emoji, tap it; To accept a highlighted suggestion by entering a space or punctuation.

• A space will appear after the suggested word is tapped. And If you enter a comma, period or other punctuation, the space will be deleted.

Suggestions can be rejected by tapping your original word (shown as the predictive text option with quotation marks).

Predictive text

Turn Off Predictive Text

1. Switch Keyboard key or Next Keyboard Emoji by holding it while editing text.

2. Slide to Keyboard Settings, and then turn off Predictive.

If you turn off predictive text, iPad 8 Gen may still try to suggest corrections for incorrect words. For you to accept a correction, you can enter a space or punctuation, or tap return. And to reject a correction, tap the "x."

Note that if you reject the same suggestion a few times, iPad 8 Gen will stop suggesting it.

Dictate text on iPad 8 Gen

On iPad 8 Gen dictate the text instead of typing it.

Note: Dictation may not be available in all languages or in all regions, and also features may vary. And Cellular data charges may apply.

Enable Dictation

1. Open Settings > General > Keyboard.

2. Turn on Enable Dictation.

Dictate Text

1. Speak when you tap the Dictate key 🎤 on the onscreen keyboard.

2. Tap the Keyboard button ⌨ when you finish

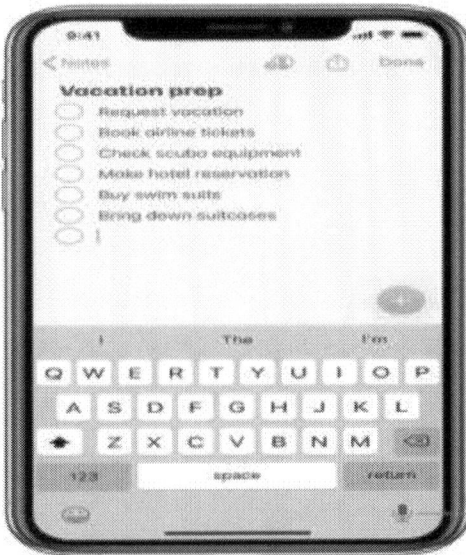

Tap to begin dictation.

To insert text by dictating, tap to place the insertion point, and then tap the Dictate key 🎤 or you can also replace selected text by dictating.

115

Add Punctuation or Format Text

Say the punctuation or formatting while dictating text

Such as "Dear Mary comma the check is in the mail exclamation mark" it will be changed to "Dear Mary, and the check is in the mail!" Punctuation and formatting commands also include the following:

- Quote end quote
- New paragraph
- New line
- Cap—to capitalize the next word
- Caps on caps off—to capitalize the first character of each word
- All caps—to make the next word all uppercase
- All caps on all caps off—to make the enclosed words all uppercase
- No caps on ... no caps off—to make the enclosed words all lowercase
- No space—to eliminate the space between two words (not available for all languages)
- No space on ... no space off—to run a series of words together (not available for all languages)
- Smiley—to insert :-)
- Frowny—to insert :-(
- Winky—to insert ;-)

Save Keystrokes On iPad 8 Gen With Text Replacements

You can Set up a text replacement or use it to enter a word or phrase by typing just a few characters and the one that is already set up for you, but you can also add your own. Type "**omw**" for example, and iPad 8 Gen will enter "On my way!"

Create a Text Replacement

1. Touch and hold the Keyboard Key or Next Keyboard Emoji while you're typing in a text field.

2. Slide to Keyboard Settings.

3. Tap Text Replacement.

4. Tap the Add button on the top right.

5. You can Type a phrase in the Phrase field above and the text shortcut you want to use for it in the Shortcut field.

Correct a Word or Phrase

Tap the Add button to create a shortcut, then enter a word or phrase in the Phrase field, but make sure to leave the Shortcut field blank.

Keep your personal dictionary up to date on your other devices, using iCloud

Open Settings > [your name] > iCloud, then turn on iCloud Drive.

Add or change keyboards on iPad 8 Gen

You can change the layout of your onscreen Keyboard, wireless Keyboard or you like to add Keyboards for writing in different languages; by turning the typing features on or off; such as spell checking.

Keyboard will automatically switch between the two languages you often use. (Not available for all languages.)

So, you can add keyboards for other languages or type in two languages without having to switch between keyboards

Set typing features

Turn special typing features— like spell check, auto-correction, and auto-capitalization— on or off, to assist your typing.

1. Open Settings > General > Keyboard or touch and hold the Next Keyboard Emoji key or switch Keyboard key while typing a text.

2. Turn special typing features on or off in the list.

Add a keyboard for another language

1. Open Settings, then tap General, then tap Keyboard > Keyboards.

2. Tap on Add New Keyboard, and then choose a keyboard.

Switch to another keyboard

1. Touch and hold the Next Keyboard Emoji key or Switch Keyboard key. While typing any text.

2. Slide your finger to the name of the keyboard you would like to choose.

To switch from one keyboard to another, you can tap the Next Keyboard Emoji key or Switch Keyboard key and also, you can continue tapping to access other enabled keyboards.

Change the keyboard layout

1. Open Settings > General > Keyboard.

2. Tap on Keyboards, select a keyboard, and then choose a layout.

Use International Keyboards on iPad 8 Gen

Open Apple's iPad 8 Gen website, choose your iPad 8 Gen, click Tech Specs, and then scroll to Languages to use international keyboards for a list of supported keyboards. And you can type text in many different languages, including Asian languages and languages written from right to left.

Manage keyboards in Settings

1. Open Settings > General > Keyboard.

2. Tap on Keyboards, and then do any of the following:

• To add a keyboard: Tap on Add New Keyboard, and then choose a keyboard from the list. You can also repeat it to add more keyboards.

• To remove a keyboard: Tap on Edit, tap the Delete button ⊖ next to the keyboard you want to remove, tap Delete, and then tap Done.

• To edit the keyboard list: Tap on Edit, drag the Reorder button ≣ next to a keyboard to a new place in the list, and then tap done.

Add an international keyboard, and the corresponding language will be automatically added to the Preferred Language Order list.

Check the list and add languages to it in Settings > General > Language & Region. You can reorder the list to change how apps and websites display text.

Add keyboards in other languages and type in two languages without having to switch between keyboards.

The keyboard will automatically switch between the two languages you often type in (Not available for all languages.)

Switch Keyboards While Typing

1. Touch and hold the Switch Keyboard button on the keyboard while typing any text.

2. Slide your finger to the name of the keyboard you would like to choose.

Tap on the Switch Keyboard button to switch from one keyboard to another and you can also continue tapping to access other enabled keyboards.

Use Accented Letters and Special Characters

You can quickly find letters and special characters on the keyboard while typing. For instance, to arrive at *é*, Long press *e*. An array of this alphabet appears on a thread above its position where you slide over to your choice.

Using alphabets and special characters is interesting judging by the wide berths of language that is on the IPad 8 Gen. For example, with a Thai keyboard, press and hold the number indicator to select native numbers. Likewise Chinese, Japanese and Arabic language, their symbols are stocked to the brim on IPad 8 Gen.

And if you are like my dad who is less techie and only communicates using our local language, press and hold the special character usually at the top of the keyboard interface, swiping to the right allows you to see and choose more options.

A point to note is that, you may decide to choose seeing fewer options, which means that you will have to do that yourself by hitting the down arrow to the right. If you prefer the full character window, click the top arrow.

Create a Text Replacement

With great intuitive text functions, using language keyboards, you can create a substitute of the original word, exercising some control over how long and short it is. After reducing it, the substitute will be saved into your IPad 8 Gen dictionary, where it frequently pops up on word suggestions.

Using a Chinese word *Pinyin* and a Japanese word *Romyi and kara,* Substitution for these indigenous languages on your phone is realised with the following set of actions:

1. Head to settings» General » Keyboard
2. Click text replacement
3. Scroll to the top and click the Aid Button $+$
4. Input the new phrase in a box that appears and include the shorter replacement in the field provided.

Reset Your Personal Dictionary

Tap settings>General>Reset. When you click reset keyboard dictionary, your customised log is erased and the keyboard dictionary returns to default.

Use special input methods on IPad 8 Gen

Your forefinger and your thumb and a stylus can create words, phrases, and characters on the IPad 8 Gen.

And you can play around with the Chinese *Cagjie* and Japanese *kara* including virtual facemasks, while flexing your creative juices with your fingers, you can create Chinese symbols in the box provided.

Build Chinese Characters from the Congjie Keys Component

Using the characters from the Congjie component is straightforward. So you are to choose a character, type it, or continue typing up to five components to see more suggestions.

Build Chinese Wubihua (Stroke) Characters

1. Use the keypad to build Chinese characters using up to five strokes, in this sequential arrangement: horizontal, vertical, left falling, right falling, and hook.

For example, the Chinese character 圈 (circle) should begin with the vertical pstroke.

2. Do any of the following:

1. As you type, suggested Chinese characters appear from device memory, usually the most commonly used characters appear first. Tap a character.

2. If you're not sure of the correct stroke, enter an asterisk (*). To see more suggestions, type another stroke, or select from the character list.

3. Tap the match key (匹配) to show only characters similar to your query.

Write Chinese Characters

Write Chinese characters directly on the screen with your finger when Simplified or Traditional Chinese handwriting input is enabled.

1. Go to Settings > General > Keyboard > Keyboards > Add New Keyboard. As you write character strokes, iPad 8 Gen recognizes them and shows matching characters and predictions above the handwriting area.

2. To enlarge the handwriting area, drag the handle above the suggestions. Tap a suggestion to use it.

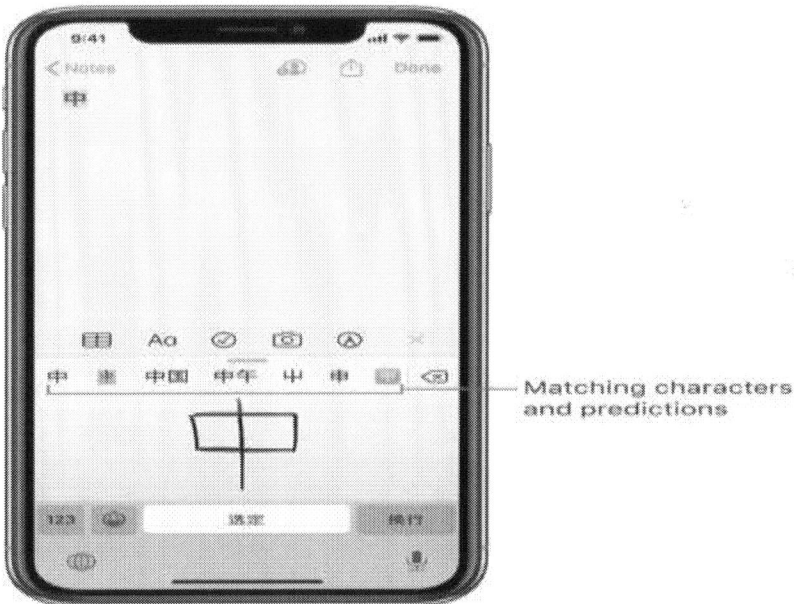

Matching characters and predictions

Type Japanese kana

Use the Kana keypad to select syllables.

For more syllable options, drag the list to the left or tap the arrow key.

Type Japanese romaji

1. Use the Romaji keyboard to type syllables. Alternative choices appear along the top of the keyboard.

2. Tap a syllable to type it.

For more syllable options, tap the arrow key and select alternatives or words from the window.

Type facemarks or emoticons

Do one of the following:

- **Use the Japanese Kana keyboard**: Tap the facemarks key ^_^ ..

- **Use the Japanese Romaji keyboard**: Tap the numbers key, then tap the facemarks key. i.e Tap .?123, and then tap ^_^ .

Using iPad 8 Gen to Search Content

Generally when you are looking for content—like applications, music, videos and files on your IPad 8 Gen, results pop up from all places; your saved applications, your gallery, your memory stick, your maps and contact are also screened by the search index. This comprehensive search function is enabled by *Siri* (more on this later).

In addition, you can adjust your application priorities and how you want to see them when they are searched. With this, you can choose the applications you like to see more often while other applications you seldomly use put on the back burner. You may want to check that out by heading to settings to set this preference.

Search with IPad 8 Gen

1. Swiftly move down on your home screen
2. Input your query by clicking the search box
3. Do any of the following
   - Collapse the keyboard interface to see larger results when you click the search button.
   - From the suggested applications, tap one of it.
   - Tap your preference to receive more information about it
   - Click your choice and voila! You are there.

- Click the **Clear text** button ⊗ in the search box to start a new search.

To begin a fresh query

1. Go to Settings>Siri>Search

2. Scroll down and Tap an app icon and Switch **show in Search on** or off.

To turn off Suggestions in Search, go to Settings , tap Siri then Search. Turn off Suggestions in Search here.

To turn off Location Services for suggestions,
1. Go to Settings, tap privacy and then choose Location Services.

2. Click System Services, then turn off Location-Based Suggestions option.

How to search in app
1. In any app, just tap the search field or button. If you don't see one, swipe down from the top.

2. Enter your text, then tap Search.

How to add a dictionary, Go to Settings, then general. Tap dictionary and select one.

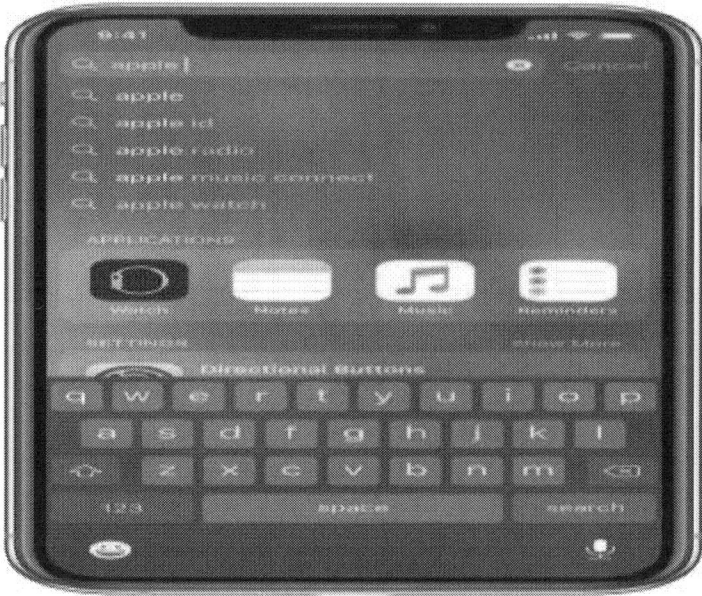

To turn off suggestions in Search

1. Hit settings

2. Move over to Siri and search

3. Then cancel suggestions in Search

Turn off location services for suggestions

1. Switching off this service is quite easy when you click settings

2. Tap **Privacy**

3. Scroll to **location services**

4. Tap system services and put an end to **Location suggestions** when you turn it off.

Search in Apps

Apart from the Siri enabled search function, traditional search box is designed to support the application allowing your favorite application to be seen and easy to navigate.

Using Maps Application

Maps provide accurate location of places including directions to unknown destinations. But a lot of people are confused with using maps that they feel lost already. Let's see how you can find a specific location.

1. In the maps application, click the search box, or button Q if you find one. If you can't find one, simply swipe down from the top.
2. Input your query and hit search.

Look around in Maps on iPad 8 Gen

View cities in the Maps app in an interactive 3D experience that lets you pan 360 degrees and move through the streets.

1. In select cities, tap the Look Around button on a map or information card.

2. To change the view, do any of the following:

- Pan: Drag a finger left or right.
- Move forward: Tap the scene.
- Zoom in or out: Pinch open or closed.
- View another point of interest: Tap elsewhere on the map.

- Switch to or from full-screen view: Tap the Enter Full Screen Mode button or the Exit Full Screen Mode button.

- Hide labels in full-screen view: Tap the information card at the bottom of the screen, then tap the Hide Labels button.

3. When finished, tap Done.

Create collections in Maps on iPad 8 Gen

In the Maps app , you can organize related places into collections for easy reference. For example, you can add destinations for an upcoming vacation into a collection named Summer Road Trip. You can quickly get to your collections from the search card, below Favorites, and you can share your collections with others.

Create a collection

Swipe up from the top of the search card, then do one of the following:

- Create one of your first three collections: Tap New Collection, enter a name, then tap Create.
- Create additional collections: When the New Collection button no longer appears, tap See All above the list of collections, tap the Add button at the bottom of the list, enter a name, tap Create, then tap the Close button.

Add a place to a collection

1. Tap a location on a map or an item in a list of search results.

2. Tap "Add to," then choose a collection.

Share a Collection

1. Swipe up from the top of the search card to show Collections, then choose a collection.

If you don't see Collections, continue swiping up.

2. Swipe up on the collection card, tap the Share button, then choose an option.

Edit a Collection

1. Swipe up from the top of the search card to show Collections, then choose a collection.

If you don't see Collections, continue swiping up.

2. Swipe up on the collection card, then tap Edit at the bottom of the screen.

3. Do any of the following:

- Rename the collection: Tap the title.
- Delete a place from the collection: Tap the place, then tap Delete at the bottom of the screen.
- Change the sort order: Tap Date Added, Name, or Distance, then choose an option.

4. Tap the Close button.

Use and Customize Control Center on iPad 8 Gen

Control Center is the preferred destination for access to advanced accessibility functions and rapid selection of handy features that you can't do without like alarm, hotspot, data e.t.c

Open Control Center

1. Drag down from the top-right edge of your IPad 8 Gen home screen

2. Swipe from the bottom of the control box to close the Control Center interface.

Access more Controls in Control Center

The functional area of the Control options are container selection that offers selective decisions over a group of specific actions.

1. Touch and hold a Control option to see its related functions. For example,

2. Long Press the cluster of controls at the top-left, click Airdrop to see other options.

Touch and hold the camera button where an interactive display opens up with take a selfie, picture or record a video functions.

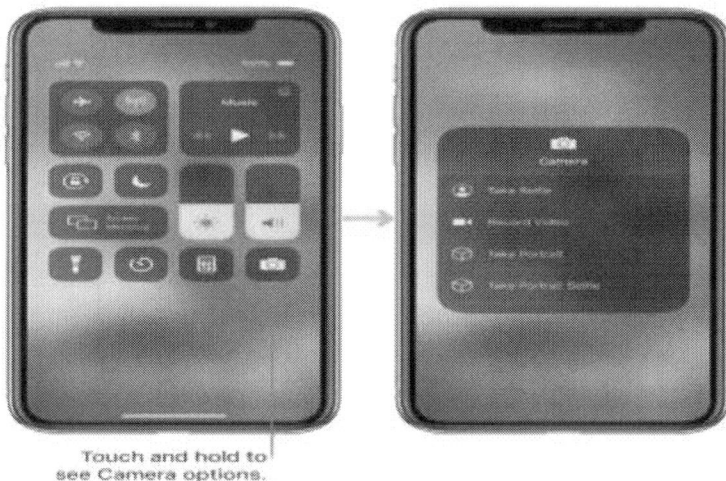

Touch and hold to
see Camera options.

Temporarily disconnect from a Wi-Fi Network

When you are surfing the net on a Wi-Fi connection that suddenly goes off, perform these actions

1. Go to Control Center
2. Manually select the Wi-Fi button as all bets on automatic connection is off.
3. Switch it on, same action goes for reconnection.

To identify the network in use— Wi-Fi here of course,

1. Long press the Wi-Fi button. This process is pretty straightforward but you may encounter minor hiccups when

you realise that your phone is still connected to a network even after disconnecting from it.

2. When your IPad 8 Gen disconnect from a network, AirPlay and AirDrop remains active in the background so that when you leave that area, your phone reconnect to a new network automatically. You can restore order by restarting your device. Go to Settings> Switch off Wi-Fi. Remember that you can also switch Wi-Fi on from the same place.

Temporary Disconnect From Bluetooth Devices

To see available Bluetooth connections;

1. Open the control center
2. Enable the Bluetooth button

Remember that temporary connection from nearby devices is usually activated by default while location services and applications continue to run in the background. In order to render Bluetooth inactive

1. Head to settings
2. Click Bluetooth
3. Switch off Bluetooth with a deft flick

While Bluetooth is used for transferring files between people, a lot of IPad 8 Gen users are not aware that exchanging data is also possible in airplane mode. Similar set of actions used for the Wi-Fi, for example, are replicated on Bluetooth activation in airplane mode.

Turn off Access to Control Center in Applications

To cancel applications access on your device, do the following;

1. Click settings
2. Go to Control Center
3. And trip off access to Control Center within applications

Add and Organize Control

To create levels of security clearance in a literal sense for your applications and the freedom, such application can exercise on your device, you should organize your applications preference. And you can achieve this purpose when you do the following;

1. Tap Settings
2. Click Control Center
3. Hit Customize Control where you start applying changes to various settings

To include special controls, from your Control Center, you can commence these changes by clicking the insert or remove function to effect these adjustments.

Apart from including and general removal of additional settings, you can do much more organization of your applications with a general shuffle function. So, drag applications icon sitting close to a Control, reorder it and place it where you want it on the screen.

View and Organize Today View on iPad 8 Gen

What Today View does is to provide personalized information. Depending on your personal, social, educational and productive choices, Today View creates a pattern for your preferences. Logical arrangement of your favorite applications, headlines, weather, calendar events, reminders and daily schedules among others.

Open Today View

To access your preferred applications;

1. Swipe from left to the opposite direction of your Home screen.

Add and Organize Today View Widgets

1. Open Today View, scroll up and
2. Hit the Edit icon at the bottom of the screen.
3. Using the insert and remove functions, choose to add or remove widgets
4. Click reorder to drag your widget preferences to a different position.

Allow access to Today View when iPad 8 Gen is locked

When you are shopping in the mall or hiking in the woods, you really want to know what is going on around you, in your world, without unlocking your device.

To quickly roam through your widgets;

1. Click Settings
2. Go to face ID, touch ID and Passcode —an intuitive access that is available on. On earlier devices, Passcode used to be the only choice.
3. Put your password
4. Switch on Today View that appears as a logical box showing **Allow access** when your IPad 8 Gen is locked.

Allow Features Access from Device Lock Screen

A lot of IPad 8 Gen users use sleek and often times unorthodox images on their lock screen. But Screen savers are one of the few features that IPad 8 Gen handles.

Quick navigation features add color to the lock screen like digital clock, day and date, network bar and battery meter just below the drag down that opens you to Control Center.

Access Features and Information from Lock Screen

Reaching your favorite features while your device is locked is quite practical;

1. Click the camera icon on your lock screen while dragging to the left to open your camera.
2. Drag down from the top-right corner.
3. Scroll up from the center of your screen to see features or widget updates and notification.
4. Drag from left to right horizontally to access Today View.

Show Notification Preview on the Lock Screen

To quickly glance through your reminders, time, widgets when you are itinerant becomes more practical with a preview.

1. Move to Settings
2. Click Notifications
3. Enable Show previews with Always function

Your messages, e-mails, calendar schedule, and social media updates are some of the notification that will fill your screen when your device is locked.

How to add widgets to the iPad Home Screen

Just as we discussed earleir, you now have the luxury of getting a lot of information at a glance as the widgets have been completely redesigned. You have the option of choosing different sizes, arrange them in any manner and add them as part of your home screen.

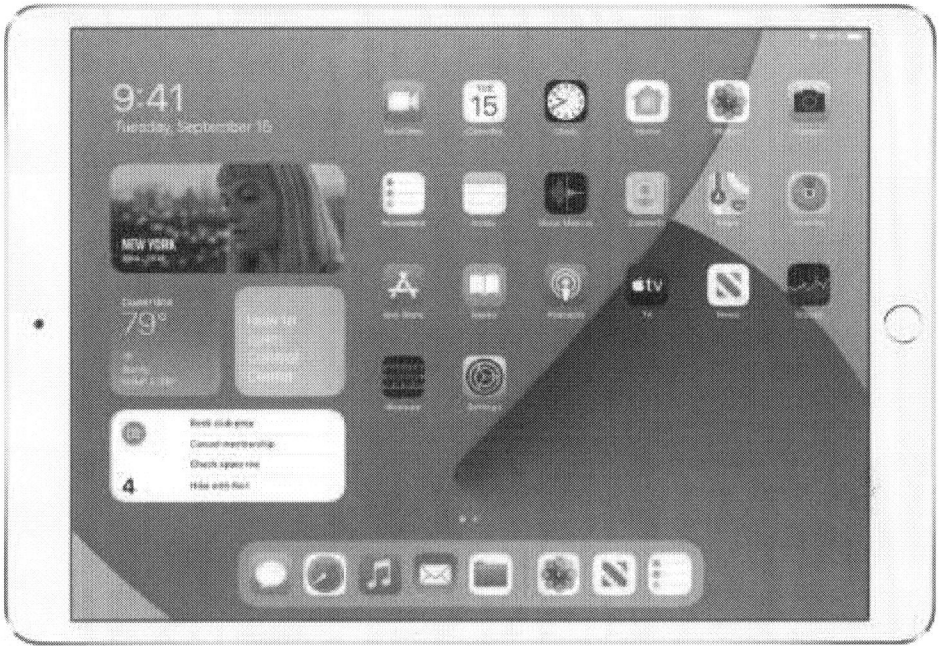

To open Today View, from the left edge of your lock or home screen, just swipe right.

How to Move a widget from Today View to the Home Screen
1. Open Today View, scroll or search to locate the widget you want.

2. Touch and hold the widget until it begins to jiggle, then drag it off the right side of the screen.

3. Drag the widget to place it where you want it on the Home Screen, then tap Done.

To add a widget to a Home Screen page;

Touch and hold the home screen at any point you wish to add the widget. Do this until you can see the apps jiggle.At the bottom of the screen, tap "Add widget". This opens the widget gallery. Choose any widget you want here and swipe left to customize the size. Choose your preferred size depending on the amount of information you want displayed and tap Done.

How to edit a widget

You can edit widgets as you wish. E.g A weather widget can be set to display forecast for any desired location. Cool thing is, you can also edit the smart stack to shuffle through its widgets based on your desired parameters.

To do this, touch and hold a widget on your home screen. A quick action menu appears where you can tap Edit. Edit as you desire and return back to home screen by a single tap.

How to Remove a widget from the Home Screen

To do this, touch and hold a widget on your home screen. A quick action menu appears where you can tap "Remove widget" or "stack" as the case may be.

To allow access to Today View when iPad is locked;

From settings, go to Face/Touch ID and passcode (depending on your phone model) and enter your code.

Just below 'allow access when locked', turn on "Today view".

142

Exploring the App Library

Swipe left past all your home screen pages to access the App library. It organizes all your apps into an easy to navigate view. Not only that, your apps are sorted into categories and the frequently used ones made just a click away.

In the App Library, you can search and open an app, expand categories and add an app to home screen. Other things you can do include:

- Perform quick actions by touching and holding an app to open a quick actions menu.
- Delete apps from your phone: touch and hold the app you wish to delete, choose delete app and tap delete.

Note: To add apps from app store to your home screen or app library, go to settings, tap home screen and click either add to App library or home screen depending on your choice. If you turn on Show in app library, app notification badge appear on apps in the library.

To hide and show Home Screen pages;

You might wish to bring the App Library closer to the first page of your Home Screen especially if you do not need many home screen pages.

So, you'll need to hide extra pages. Touch and hold an app on the home screen, tap edit. You'll see dots at the bottom of the home screen. Tap them. You'll see thumbnails of your home pages. Tap to remove the checkmarks below the thumbnails of pages you wish to hide. To show the pages again, just tap to add the check marks again. Press done or the home button twice (depending on your phone model).

How to use app clips on iPad

An app clip allows you to quickly perform certain tasks in an app without downloading and installing the full app. When you need a small part of an app to focus on specific tasks e.g ordering a meal or bike renting, App clip is your plug.

It can be found in messages, safari or maps. When you see an app clip link, tap and scan the QR code shown at the physical location with your camera.

Lastly, bring your phone near the near-field communications (NFC) tag and the app clip card appears at the bottom of the screen. You can also pay for the app using Apple pay in supported app clips.

To find an app clip you recently used on your phone, Go to App Library, then click Recently Added. To remove app clips, Go to Settings, tap App Clips, and then choose Remove All App Clips.

How to translate voice and text on iPad

You can have conversations easily with this app by translating using voice or text. Simply put the orientation of your phone in landscape if you wish to enter a conversation mode. You also have the option to download your favorite languages and save your favorite translations.

Translating Text or Voice

Orient your phone to portrait mode and tap Translate. Select the languages at the top of the screen. You can now enter a text or say a phrase by tapping the listen button. As soon as you get the translation; you can save it, look up a word in the dictionary by tapping the dictionary button then the word and you can also replay translation audio.

How to translate a conversation

You do not need internet connection for downloaded languages. Put your phone in landscape by rotating and tap the listen button. Speak and your words will be transcribed on one side of the split screen.

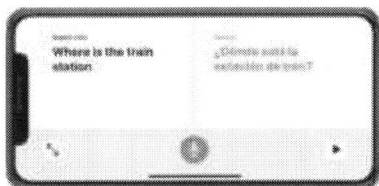

How to get someone's Attention With Large Text

Tap the broadcast mode button In the Translate tab after you must have rotated your phone to landscape.,

If you wish to download languages to iPad for offline translation, after you tap the translate bar, choose a language at the top of the screen. Scroll to the desired language and press done.

Choose iPad 8 Gen Settings for Travel

Being aware of roaming charges when you are travelling as this could save you from data fees. Also try to know about the airline policy on air, as this will determine your safety too.

Switch your device to Airplane mode when the airline you are boarding allows the use of smartphones and other electrical devices in transit. Airplane mode deactivates calls, internet and Bluetooth. When these functions remain inactive, you can use your device for multimedia purposes like music, and movies.

Activate Airplane Mode

Drag down the Control Center from the right, when the interface opens;

- Click the Airplane mode

From the settings logical box, usually on the status bar, flip on the Airplane mode that appears as an aeroplane.

Switch On Bluetooth and Wi-Fi Using Airplane Mode

Provided that airline procedures encourage it, activate Wi-Fi and Bluetooth in Airplane mode.

1. Go over to Control Center
2. Enable Airplane mode
3. In the same box, enable Wi-Fi and Bluetooth directly from their icons

When the plane touchdown, and you had a wonderful or cranky flight, you are often concerned with necessary clearance and less bothered about your device. Bluetooth and Wi-Fi remain active requiring that you manually disable it on the Control Center.

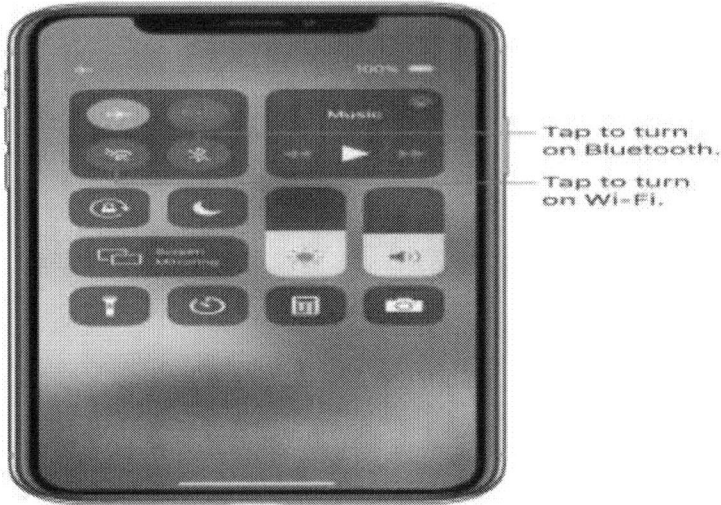

View Your Screen Time Summary on iPad 8 Gen

Screen Time allows you to see your log activities. This is a work of genius that shows how your device performed over a period of time.

This performance data allows you to benchmark your favorite applications and identify malicious activities of other less-used programs.

You can also create a time management schedule to reduce and control time spent on your device, creating priorities for applications and favorite websites.

Setting up Screen time is pretty easy where a description profile is created for your device that includes;

1. Time breakdown on application basis especially with categories like social media, entertainment, productivity e.t.c
2. Daytime performance data of each application.
3. Time log of each application, including applications that stretched beyond the time cap.
4. Detailed tracking of notifications, including the applications that pop up more frequently than others on the notification panel.
5. A timeline of applications accessed when you unlock your device.

Going over each application in your Screen time Summary allows you to go into more details. When you have concluded your Screen time profile;

1. View your login Settings
2. Tap Screen time
3. Hit See all activity

Congratulations! You can now benchmark your device's usage over days and weeks.

Setting up a Personal ScreenTime

Screen time allows you to attach freedom and privileges to applications and restrict the activities of various applications. You can set permissions and limits for applications, including a downtime schedule e.t.c These settings can be reviewed and cancelled as you wish.

Creating a Downtime Schedule

You don't have to worry about unhealthy phone habits that are quite evident with people living their lives practically on the phone, an addiction of some sort when a downtime schedule is created. Downtime has to do with your off-the-phone activities allowing your device to rest.

When your phone is idle, you can take charge of your time and spend it with people or projects that matters to you. This time management system ensures that you take control of applications that you want to see and how much freedom they can exercise.

1. Click Settings
2. Tap Screen Time
3. Click Turn on Screen Time when it is off by default
4. Tap continue
5. Click "This is my phone"
6. Scroll down to Downtime
7. Enable Downtime
8. Customize preferences showing occurrence and time lapse with begin and end schedule

Setting Applications Limit

Set entertainment and productivity limits for applications category

1. Go to settings
2. Click Screen Time
3. Enable Turn on Screen Time
4. Hit Continue
5. Tap *This is my Phone*
6. Tap App limits
7. Add App limits

8. Replicate on other application categories.

Applying application limits without first isolating it from it's category, issuing command or instruction on other applications.

1. Tap next to include hours and minutes

2. Tap Customize days to create daily limits and include time structure for important days.

3. To create a scheme for applications limit in categories, click Choose Apps.

4. Return to the App limits window after clicking Add.

To switch off app limits for a short time;

1. Tap App limits

2. Under app limits options, attach a short break for specific application and those in a category.

In addition, for clustered applications existing in a category;

1. Tap category

2. Click Application limit and set short time intervals

3. Tap Delete limit to effect new changes.

Setting Allowed Applications

IPad 8 Gen knows that you have a preference for certain applications that you can't do without. Your maps bursting your favourite destinations and other productive tools. So you might create a schedule that keeps these applications running at all times. To do this;

1. Jump to Settings
2. Click Screen Time.
3. Enable Screen Time
4. Click Continue where your
5. screen pops This is my Phone window.
    1. Enable Always Allowed
    1. Click Add or Delete function to add and remove applications on the Allowed Apps list.

Set Content and Privacy Restrictions

You can further be in charge of your content when you set boundaries on the applications you wish to see on the Apple's Store including ITunes recommendations.

1. Go to Settings
2. Click Screen Time
3. Tap Turn on Screen Time
4. Click Continue when you are taken to **This is my IPad 8 Gen** window.
5. Enable Content and Restriction when you click Content and Privacy restrictions
6. Select options provided and apply changes to specific contents.

Just like how security clearance is used in big organizations, allowing and restricting people to information, Content and privacy also provides the same levels of freedom.

This action creates a ceiling for the iTunes store, apps, content ratings, and Apple store recommendations.

Attach a password to create a valid access, which is important to change settings in the future. Sharing your Screen Time reports and settings, including device synchronization is easier on the internet and iPad 8 Gen community when you sign in with your Apple account.

Set up Screen Time for a Family Member on iPad 8 Gen

Creating a schedule for applications is more interesting when you can extend the same privilege to your folks and family. Using Screen Time for family requires that family sharing is active on your IPad 8 Gen, the changes become evident on their devices.

Set Downtime and Applications Limit On a Family Device

In order to place strict measures for your children who have an iPad 8 Gen, take a little time to set downtime and limit how much they use their device. On their device, do the following;

1. Click settings
2. Tap Screen Time
3. Enable Turn on Screen Time
4. Click Continue
5. Scroll up and tap **This is my child's phone**

Create a downtime structure for entertainment and social applications with time intervals

1. Click downtime
2. For creating limits for applications in categories, click categories
3. Tap Show all
4. Scroll through each application and establish limit conditions
5. Click Set App limit when you are done
6. Tap continue with a Screen Time password to access your folk's Screen Time settings subsequently

Choose Allowed Apps on a Family Member Device

While it is possible to create downtime and applications limit on your child's device, you can also create an invariable allowed app profile that cannot be easily changed without permission. To adjust Screen Time setting for your folks where you are the de facto system administrator, selecting set of applications they use can be achieved with the following process;

1. Click Settings

2. Tap Screen Time on their device

3. Choose Always allowed

4. Create and adjust their application preference with Add or Delete function. Ensure that you don't put your children or folks in harm when you leave out applications using downtime settings that are a lifesaver like emergency call.

5. So that your intentions don't backfire, include these applications in the Allowed list where it can exercise overlap on downtime privileges after time interval elapsed.

Set Content and Privacy Restrictions on a

Reduce the consumption of inappropriate content by your folks, ensuring adequate privacy settings for their age.

To achieve this;

1. Click settings

2. Tap Screen Time

3. Enable Content and Privacy restrictions

4. Create content and privacy profile

5. When you are done, tap Back button

Add or Change Screen Time Settings for A Family Member Later

Using the same Screen Time set-up process, replicate it for your family much later. Note that in the event were you forget the password used to set-up this settings on their device, take the following action if you created a profile on the family sharing option;

1. Erase IPad 8 Gen memory
2. Restore backup from icloud or iTunes

Similarly, Family sharing settings can work both ways where you implement it from your own device. When you create a profile on your IPad 8 Gen, you directly control application permissions for them at will. When you lose the pass code to these Settings, nothing stops you from adding and removing content, using your device pattern, Face ID or touch ID.

Monitor Device Performance

With Screen Time set up and in place, knowing how your IPad 8 Gen is performing becomes easier;

1. Go to Settings
2. Tap Screen Time
3. Click See All Activity to catch a glance on your weekly charts
4. Click Day to access daily rankings

Keeping tabs on your device performance is more convenient when you include a widget for Screen Time on the Today View. If you don't want your Today View window to be cluttered with too much, go to Screen Time weekly Report notification on your home screen.

Charge and Monitor the Battery

IPad 8 Gen uses a lithium-ion, non-removable battery. Lithium batteries are industry standard power capacities that are relatively lighter, durable and charges quickly with a huge battery-shelf life.

Charge the Battery

Plug your IPad 8 Gen to a power outlet, using two options — fast USB cable and USB adaptor. While revving up your IPad 8 Gen batteries, constantly check the battery bar where it beeps intermittently.

When you are not charging your IPad 8 Gen with an adaptor but with a cable attached to a computer, ensure that the computer remains in active mode to increase the strength of your batteries.

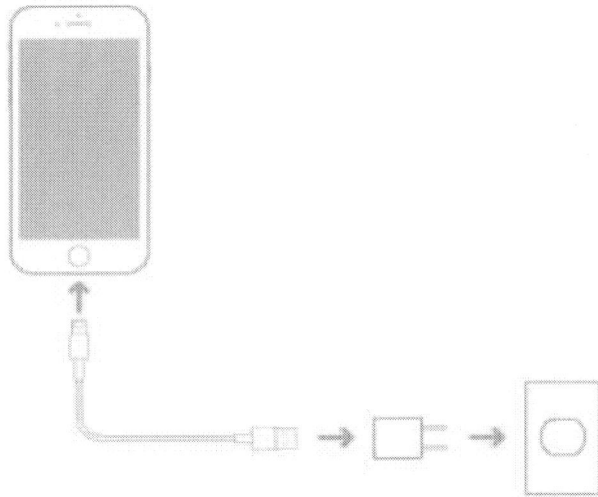

Connect iPad 8 Gen to a USB port on your computer, which also allows you to sync iPad 8 Gen with iTunes. Make sure your computer is turned on—if the iPad 8 Gen is connected to a computer that's turned off, the battery may drain instead of charge. Look for the charging icon on the battery icon to make sure your iPad 8 Gen is charging.

With recent advances in technology, charging IPad 8 Gen has become more innovative where you can power your device with a Qi-certified charger. Put your device on the charger, leaving it to charge.

Similarly, this charging technology enables you to access ITunes synchronization automatically and an unsolicited icloud backup. Don't attempt to charge your device with low voltage auxiliary devices like keyboard unless they are USB lightning variant.

The battery icon in the upper-right corner shows the battery level or charging status.

When you synchronize your device, blast music or watch movies, battery charges very slowly. So you might want to stop your device usage especially when the power is almost gone.

When your device is almost dead, the battery bar is red, requiring a quick 10 minutes power bust. When it is quite low, the display is blank for about 120 seconds and the battery-low image blinks intermittently on the Lock screen.

WARNING: Refrain from charging your device with the Lightning cable connection when you observe that a liquid content in the connector.

Show the Percentage of Battery Remaining in the Status Bar

To make battery percentage visible on New iPad 8 Gen, swipe down horizontally from the right.

Turn on Low Power Mode

When your device is on Low Power Mode, charging your phone is really fast but your phone performance could take some cost of this action. Use Low Power Mode when you want to conserve battery energy and your IPad 8 Gen power is completely on the ebb.

1. Click settings
2. Enable Low Power Mode on Battery

Low Power Mode limits background activity and tune performance for essential tasks like making and receiving calls, email, and messages; accessing the Internet; and more.

Note: If your iPad 8 Gen switches to Low Power Mode automatically, it switches back to normal power mode after charging to 80%. Your iPad 8 Gen might perform some tasks more slowly when in Low Power Mode.

View Your Battery Usage Information

Go to Settings > Battery.

Your battery dossier shows daily activities for 10 days where details about activity, battery-eating applications, insights and suggestions among others are provided.

Information about your battery usage and activity appears for the last 24 hours and up to the last 10 days.

Insights and suggestions: Specific details about how your battery ranks with tough demands from applications and system settings are shown including suggestions that helps you manage energy. When a suggestion appears, tap it to change settings.

Last Charge Level: shows battery charge status including time records of discontinued charging.

Battery Level graph (in Last 24 Hours): provides details on the battery level, discontinued charge and periods when iPad 8 Gen was in Low Power Mode.

Battery Usage graph (over 10 Days): Shows the dossier of battery used each, daily in percentage.

Activity graph: indicates activity over time, showing both active and idle records.

Screen On and Screen Off: provides data about total activity for the selected time interval, during active and inactive moments. The Last 10 Days view provides average daily reports.

Battery Usage by App: Shows the percentage of battery power utilised by each app in the selected time interval.

Activity by App: Shows the amount of time each app was used in the selected time interval.

If you are concerned about specific hours or days, check battery information and select the period on the graph. To go back to the full report, tap outside the area.

Check Your Battery's Health

1. Go to Settings > Battery.

2. Tap Battery Health.

When you check battery health, iPad 8 Gen displays data about your battery's capacity, peak performance, applications that gulps bigger battery power and whether your battery needs to be maintained. Eventually, with time, a battery begin to relapse, losing its strength. When your batteries are out, find an Apple authorized Service Provider to replace or optimise performance.

Optimize iPad 8 Gen Battery Charging

iPad 8 Gen has a setting that helps slow the rate of your battery's shelflife, reducing charging time. Using artificial intelligence algorithms, this Settings allows you to understand your daily charging routine, stalls around 80% ending up in your battery dossier. To set this up;

1. Click Settings > Battery, and tap Battery Health.

2. Enable Optimized Battery Charging.

Learn the Meaning of the iPad 8 Gen Status Icons

The icons in the status bar at the top of the screen provide information about iPad 8 Gen. On New iPad 8 Gen, there are additional status icons at the top of Control Center.

Cell signal : The number of bars shows you the signal strength of your network provider When the bar is empty, "No Service" appears.

Dual cell signals: On models with Dual SIM, network bars are duplicated, the one above shows the signal strength of the cellular data SIM while the other one indicates the signal strength of your other line. If there's no signal, "No Service" appears. To identify network providers with their relative brand, tap the control center.

Airplane mode: Switching Airplane mode disables the network providers and other wireless functions.

LTE : When your network carrier's LTE is available, iPad 8 Gen connects to the world and open you to remote personalized services on that Carrier which is not available in all regions.

5G E : Your device's 5G E network is available and supported on IPad 8 Gen 8 and subsequent releases but with few regions enjoying 5G service, you might be restricted when your location does not allow this service.

UMTS : This 4G UMTS (GSM) or LTE network (depending on the carrier) comes with this device, its application largely depends on the region.

UMTS/EV-DO: Your carrier's 3G UMTS (GSM) or EV-DO (CDMA) network is available, and iPad 8 Gen can connect to the Internet over that network.

EDGE : Your carrier's EDGE (GSM) network is available, and iPad 8 Gen can connect to the Internet over that network.

GPRS/1xRTT : Your carrier's GPRS (GSM) or 1xRTT (CDMA) network is available, and iPad 8 Gen can connect to the Internet over that network.

Wi-Fi call: iPad 8 Gen is set up for Wi-Fi calling. iPad 8 Gen also displays a carrier name next to the icon.

Wi-Fi: iPad 8 Gen is connected to the Internet over a Wi-Fi network. See Connect iPad 8 Gen to a Wi-Fi network.

The Personal Hotspot status icon.

Personal Hotspot iPad 8 Gen is connected to the Internet when another device acts as a modem

Personal Hotspot Indicator : A blue bubble frequently glows on the IPad 8 Gen is an indicator that a Personal Hotspot, Screen Mirroring and a background application is using your location.

Call Indicator : A green bubble or bar indicates the iPad 8 Gen is on a call.

Recording Indicator : A red bubble or bar indicates the iPad 8 Gen is either recording sound or recording your screen.

CarPlay: iPad 8 Gen is connected to CarPlay.

Syncing : iPad 8 Gen is syncing with iTunes.

Network activity: Shows that there's network activity. Some third-party apps may also use it to show an active process.

Call Forwarding: Call Forwarding is active

VPN: You're connected to a network using VPN and using one yourself.

TTY: Software RTT / TTY or Hardware TTY is turned on.

Lock: iPad 8 Gen is locked.

Do Not Disturb: Do Not Disturb is enabled

Portrait orientation lock: The iPad 8 Gen screen is locked in portrait orientation.

Location Services: An application is using Location Services leaving it running in the background.

Alarm: An alarm has been set.

Headphones connected: iPad 8 Gen is paired with Bluetooth enabled headphones that are turned on and within Bluetooth range.

Bluetooth battery : Shows the battery percentage of a paired Bluetooth device.

Battery: Shows the iPad 8 Gen battery position and clearly indicates phone performance. When the icon turns yellow, that means Low Power Mode is active.

Battery Charging: Shows from the beeping icon that the iPad 8 Gen battery

Chapter 7: Switching Between Apps on iPad 8 Gen

Launch the App Switcher to switch from one app to another on your iPad 8 Gen. You can start from where you stopped when you switch back.

Making use of the App Switcher

1. To access all your open apps in the App Switcher, you can get the following done:
*   Go to the bottom edge of your device, swipe up and pause at the center of the screen.

To browse all open apps: Swipe to the right and select the app you like to use.

Switching Between Open Apps

Swipe left or right along the bottom edge of your device's screen to switch quickly between open apps.

Moving and organizing apps on iPad 8 Gen

Apps can be rearranged on your device, organized in folders as well as get them moved to other pages or screens. Pages can also be reordered.

Moving apps around the Home screen into the Dock or other pages

1. Go to your device's Home screen.

2. Touch and hold an app on the device's Home screen until the app icons jiggle.

3. Get an app dragged to one of the following locations:

• A different location on the same page.
• Dock located at the bottom of the screen.

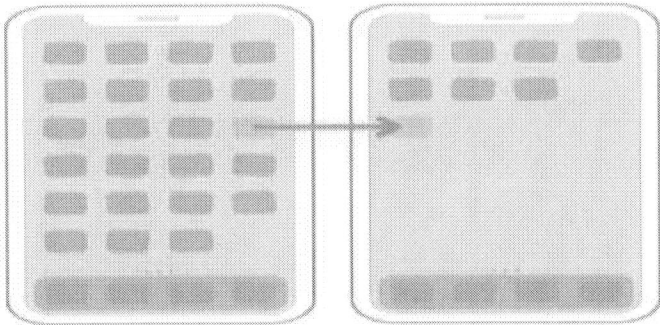

• Drag the app to the right edge of the screen to access a different page. Once you do this, you might need to wait for a few seconds for the new page to show up. Note that the dots available above the Dock indicate how many pages you have and the one you are currently viewing.

Creating Folders and Organizing Your Apps

Apps can be grouped in your folders to help access them more easily from your Home screen. To do this, you are required to take the following steps:

1. Go to your device's Home screen.

2. Touch and hold an app on the device's Home screen until the app icons jiggle.

3. Drag an app onto another app to get a folder created.

4. Select and drag other apps into the folder created in the previous step. Note that you can have multiple pages of apps in the folder.

5. Tap the name field and enter a new name to get the folder renamed.

6. Select DONE.

Note: To get a folder deleted, all you need to do is drag all the apps out of the folder and the folder will be deleted automatically.

How to Reset the Home Screen and Apps To Their Original Layout

1. Go to Settings.

2. Select "General."

3. Select "Reset."

4. Tap on "Reset Home Screen Layout"

Once these instructions are correctly followed, any folder you must have created will be removed and the apps that have been downloaded will get alphabetically ordered following the apps that came with your iPad 8 Gen.

Removing Apps from iPad 8 Gen

Apps can be removed from your iPad 8 Gen if the need arises and they can be downloaded back later when you change your mind.

Removing Apps from the Home Screen

1. Go to your device's Home screen.

2. Touch and hold an app on the device's Home screen until the app icons jiggle.

3. Tap the Close button icon on the app to be removed.

4. Tap "Delete."

5. Select DONE.

Note that every app removed can be re-downloaded at any time if you change your mind.

Apart from getting third-party apps removed, the following built-in Apple apps that came with your iPad 8 Gen can also be removed:

- Books
- Calculator
- Calendar
- Home
- iTunes Store
- Compass

- Contacts: It is to be noted that the contact information will remain available via Messages, Phone, Mail, FaceTime including other apps. Contacts must be restored to get a contact removed.
- FaceTime
- Files
- Shortcuts
- Stocks
- Tips
- Find My
- Mail
- Maps
- TV
- Voice Memos
- Watch
- Measure
- Music
- News
- Notes
- Podcasts
- Reminders
- Weather

Note: Related user data and configuration files will also be removed when you remove a built-in app from the Home screen.

It is also important to note that, other system functionality can be affected when built-in apps are removed from your Home screen.

Keeping Your Favorite Apps Readily Available On iPad 8 Gen

Your favorite apps can be kept in such a way that they will be easily accessible in the Control center or Today view on your iPad 8 Gen.

• The Control Center gives easy access to apps such as Notes or Voice Memos.

• In Today View, widgets are used to provide timely information from your apps at a glance.

Customizing the Control Center to include your favorite apps

Shortcuts can be added to apps such as Calendar, Voice Memos, Notes, Wallet and many more. To do this, you are required to take the following steps:

1. Go to Settings.

2. Select "Control Center."

3. Select "Customize Controls."

4. Tap the Insert button which is next to each app to be added.

Adding widgets in Today View

Information can be derived from your favorite apps at a glance. Do this by selecting from Maps Nearby, Notes, Calendar, News, Reminders and many more. To do this, you are required to take the following steps:

1. Go to the Home screen.
2. Open "Today View" by swiping right.
3. Scroll to the bottom.
4. Select "Edit"
5. Tap on the insert button which is next to each app to be added.
6. Select "Done"

TIP: For traffic conditions to be included for your commute in Today View, take the following steps:

1. Go to Settings.
2. Select "Privacy"
3. Select "Location Services"
4. Tap on "System services"
5. Tap on "Significant Locations"
6. Turn on Significant Locations.

Performing quick actions from the Home screen

Open quick action menus by going to the Home screen after which you can touch and hold app icons.

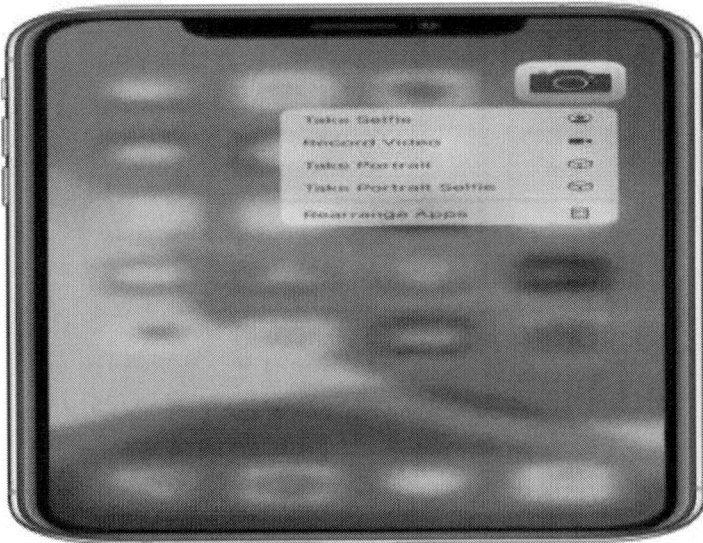

Examples:

- **Taking a selfie:** Touch and hold "Camera" and select "Take Selfie."

- **Accessing your location:** Touch and hold "Map" and select "Send My Location."

- **New Note:** Touch and hold "Notes" and select "New Note."

It is to be noted that if an app icon is touched and held for too long before getting to select a quick action, the icons will start to jiggle. Once this happens, tap done.

Chapter 8: Get Apps, Games, and Font in the App Store on iPad 8 Gen

The App Store provides a platform where you can get to discover new apps and games, get custom fonts downloaded and learn about tips and tricks.

The App store also enables you to subscribe to Apple Arcade which is not available in all regions or countries. New games can also be accessed on your iPad 8 Gen, iPhone, Mac, iPod touch and Apple TV.

Finding Apps, Games, and Fonts

Ask Siri by saying something like "Search the App Store for cooking apps" or "Get the Minecraft app."

Tap on any of the following:

- **Today:** With this, you get to discover all featured stories and apps.
- **Games or Apps:** Use this feature to explore new releases, view top charts or browse using categories.
- **Arcade:** This feature enables you to subscribe to Apple Arcade as well as gaining access to new games on your iPad 8 Gen, iPad 8 Gen, iPod touch, Apple TV and Mac.
- **Search:** With this feature, you can search for anything you are looking for by tapping on Search on the keyboard.

177

Buy and Download An App

1. Tap the price to purchase an app.

2. Tap Get if the app is free.

3. For an app that has already been purchased, a download button will come up instead of a price and get it re-downloaded without having to pay for it.

4. Authenticate your Apple ID using the Face ID, Touch ID or passcode to get a purchase completed if you are prompted.

Note that once an app is downloading, it will come up on the Home screen with a progress indicator.

Give or Redeem an App Store and ITunes Gift Card

1. Select the My Account button or your profile picture which is located at the top right.

2. Choose from one of the following options.

- Redeem gift card or code

- Send gift card via email

It is important to note that an internet connection, as well as an Apple ID, will be needed to make use of the App Store. The App Store availability and its features vary based on countries or regions.

Manage Your App Store Purchases, Subscriptions, and Settings on iPad 8 Gen

• You can get to manage your subscriptions as well as reviewing and downloading purchases that you made or were made by other family members in the App Store app.

• Your preference for App Store in Settings can also be customized.

Approve Purchases Using Family Sharing

Family sharing can be set up for the family organizer to review and approve purchases that are made by other family members under a certain age.

View and re-download eligible apps purchased by you or family members

1. Select the My Account button or your profile picture which is located at the top right.

2. Select "Purchased"

3. Tap "My Purchases" or select a family member to view their purchases if you had set up Family Sharing.

4. Search for the app you like to download.

5. Tap on the "Download button"

Note: You can only get to see purchases made by family members if they decide to share their purchases. The purchases that were made with the Family sharing set up may become inaccessible once the family member leaves the family group.

Manage Your Subscriptions

1. Select the My Account button or your profile picture which is located at the top right.
2. Select "Subscriptions"

Changing your App Store settings

1. Go to Settings.
2. Select [your name].
3. Select "iTunes & App Store"
4. You can perform any of the following actions:

- Automatically get apps purchased downloaded on your Apple devices: Do this by going below Automatic Downloads and turning on Apps

- Automatically update apps: This feature enables you to turn on your App updates.

- Control the use of cellular data for app downloads: Turn on Automatic Downloads to allow downloads to make use of cellular data. Tap "App Downloads," to choose if you want to be asked for downloads permission which are over 200 MB or all apps.

- Automatically play app preview videos: Get the Video Autoplay turned on.

Chapter 9: Drawing in apps with Markup on iPad 8 Gen

The built-in drawing tools can be used to annotate photos, screenshots, PDFs and many more for supported apps such as Mail, Messages, Notes, and Books.

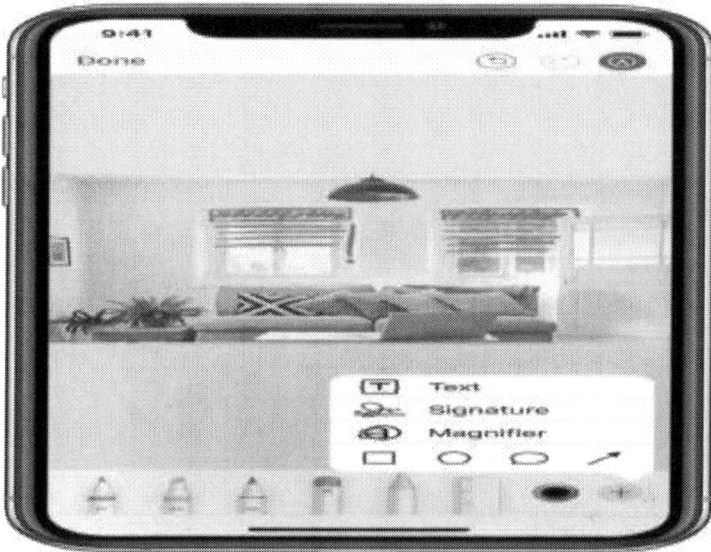

Drawing with Markup

1. Tap on the Markup Switch button off or Markup for supported apps.

2. Go to the Markup toolbar.

2. Tap pen, marker or pencil tool.

4. Write or draw using your finger.

5. Tap the Markup Switch button or select Done to hide the Markup toolbar.

6. In the process of drawing you can carry out any of the following actions:

- Change the line weight: To do this, Tap on the drawing tool available in the toolbar and select an option.
- Change the opacity: Do this by tapping the drawing tool in the toolbar and drag the slider.
- Change the color: This can be done by tapping on the Color Picker button which is available in the toolbar after which you can then select a color.
- Undo a mistake: Select the Undo button.
- Draw a straight line: Go to the toolbar and select the ruler tool. Then get a line drawn along the ruler edge.
- Change the angle of the ruler: Do this by touching and holding the ruler using your two fingers and rotate your fingers afterward.
- Moving the ruler without changing its angle: Do this by dragging it with one finger instead of two fingers.
- To make the ruler disappear: Make the ruler tool disappear by tapping on the ruler tool again.

Erasing a Mistake

Go to the Markup toolbar in a supported app and select the eraser tool. Once this is done, you can perform the following actions:

- Erasing with the pixel eraser: Make use of your finger in scrubbing over the mistake.

- Erasing with the object eraser: Make use of your finger to touch the object.

- Switching between the pixel and the object erasers: Select the eraser tool again and choose between the Pixel Eraser or Object Eraser.

Note: Tap the Markup Switch button off or Markup if the Markup toolbar doesn't come up. Tap on its minimized version if the toolbar is minimized.

Moving Elements of Your Drawing

1. Go to the Markup toolbar.

2. Select the Lasso tool which is in between the eraser and ruler tools.

3. To make a selection, drag around the elements.

4. Release your finger.

5. Get your selection dragged to a new location.

Note: You can mark up a screenshot immediately after it is taken by tapping the thumbnail which will appear for a few moments at the bottom left corner of the screen. Share your screenshot after it is marked up by tapping on the Share button.

Adding text, shapes, as well as, signatures using Markup on iPad 8 Gen

Markup can be used to add texts, shapes, speech bubbles and signatures for supported apps.

Adding text

1. For the supported app, go to the Markup toolbar.

2. Select the "Add Annotation button"

3. Tap "Text"

4. Double-tap on the text box.

5. Make use of the keyboard to input text.

6. Edit text after it is been added by tapping on the text to select it and perform any of the following actions:

- Change the size, font or layout: To do this, select the "Shape Attributes button" in the toolbar and select your preferred option.
- Deleting, editing or duplicating text: Tap on Edit and select an option.
- Move the text: Drag the text to get it moved.
-

Adding a shape

1. For the supported app, go to the Markup toolbar.

2. Select the "Add Annotation button"

3. Select a shape.

4. To get the shape adjusted, you can perform any of the following actions:

- Move the shape: Drag the shape to get it moved.
- Resize the shape: Do this by dragging any blue dot available along the shape's outline.
- Change the outline color: Go to the color picker and select a color.
- Get the shape filled with color or change the line thickness: Select the Shapes Attribute button and select your preferred option.
- Adjusting the form of an arrow or speech bubble shape: Do this by dragging a green dot.
- Delete or get a shape duplicated: Select this and choose your preferred option.

1. Hide the Markup toolbar when done by tapping the Markup Switch button on or Done.

Adding your signature

1. For the supported app, go to the Markup toolbar.

2. Select the "Add Annotation button"

3. Select "Signature."

4. If the Markup toolbar doesn't show up, select the Markup Switch button off or Markup.

5. Hide the Markup toolbar when done by tapping the Markup Switch button on or Done.

Zoom In or Magnify in Markup on iPad 8 Gen

For supported apps, zoom in to get details drawn in Markup. The magnifier should only be used when you need to get details viewed.

Zoom in

- Pinch open so you can get to draw, adjust shapes and many more while making use of the Markup for the supported app.
- Drag two fingers to the pan when you are zoomed in and pinch close to zoom back out.

Magnify

1. For the supported app, go to the Markup toolbar.

2. Select the "Add Annotation button"

3. Select "Magnifier"

4. If the Markup toolbar doesn't show up, select the Markup Switch button off or Markup.

5. Change the characteristics of the magnifier by doing any of the following:

- Changing the magnification level: To do this, drag the green dot available on the magnifier.

- Change the size of the magnifier: Do this by dragging the blue dot on the magnifier.

- Move the magnifier: Drag the magnifier to do this.

- Changing the outline thickness of the magnifier: Tap the "Shapes Attribute button" and select an option.

- Changing the outline color of the magnifier: Select an option from the color picker.

- Removing or duplicating the magnifier: Select its outline and tap on Delete or Duplicate.

1. Hide the Markup toolbar when done by tapping the Markup Switch button on or Done.

Installing and Managing App Extensions on iPad 8 Gen

With some apps, you can extend the functionality of your iPad 8 Gen. An app extension can appear in the form of any of the following:

- A sharing option
- An action option
- A widget in Today View
- File provider
- A custom keyboard

The App extensions can also be used for editing a photo or video in your Photos app. An example of this is downloading a photo-related app to get filters applied to your photos.

Downloading and Installing App Extensions

1. Go to the App Store.

2. Download the app.

3. Launch the app.

4. Follow the onscreen instructions that come up.

Managing Sharing or Action Options

1. Select the Share button.

2. Tap More. Note that you may need to swipe the options to get the More option revealed.

3. Turn on or off the "Sharing or action" options.

4. Touch and drag the Reorder button to reorder the options.

5. Select "Done"

Move Items with Drag and Drop on Your iPad 8 Gen

A finger can be used to move text as well as other items within an app using the drag and drop feature. This feature also comes in handy in doing the following:

- Getting a list in the Reminders app rearranged.

- Moving a text selection or a photo in Notes.
- Drag an event to a new time slot in the Calendar app.

However, it is important to note that not all third-party apps support the drag and drop feature.

Moving Text

1. Go to the text editing app.

1. Select the text you like to move.
2. Once selected touch and hold the text until it lifts.

3. Get it dragged to another location within the app. Note that if you drag it to the top or bottom of a long document, it will automatically scroll in either direction.

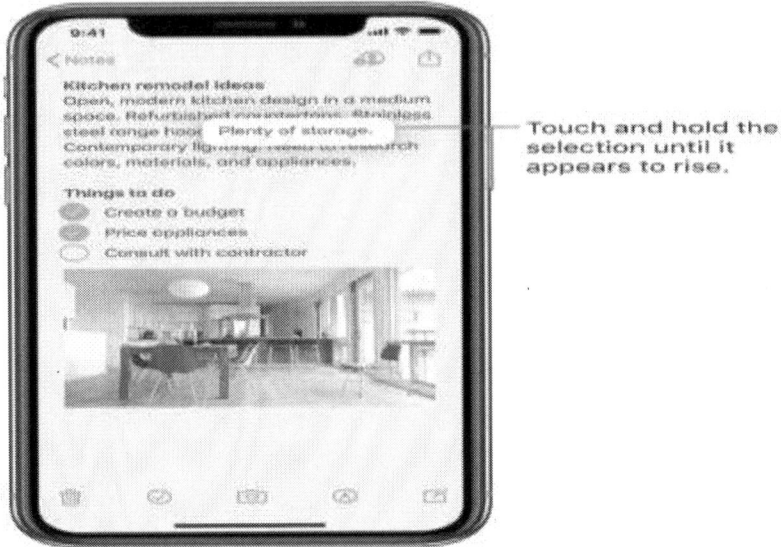

Touch and hold the selection until it appears to rise.

Note: You can lift your finger before dragging or drag an item off the screen if you decide not to move the text again.

Select Multiple Items to Move

1. Touch and hold the initially selected item.

2. Get it dragged slightly and keep holding.

3. While the first item is being held, use another finger to tap additional items.

4. A badge will indicate the number of selected items.

5. Get all the items dragged together.

Note: You can lift your finger before dragging or drag an item off the screen if you decide not to move the text again.

Using Airdrop on the iPad 8 Gen to Send Items to Devices close To You

- AirDrop enables you to wirelessly send videos, photos, locations, websites and many more to other devices or Mac computers that are nearby.
- The AirDrop gets the information transferred making use of the Wi-Fi and Bluetooth with both turned on.
- You must be signed in to your Apple ID to make use of the AirDrop and it is to be noted that all transfers made are encrypted for security measures.

Sending an   Item Using Airdrop

1. Open the item to be transferred.

2. Select the Share button, Share, AirDrop, More options button or any other button that shows the sharing options of the app.

3. Then, you can do one of the following:

4. Select the AirDrop icon available in the row of share options after which you can select the profile picture of an AirDrop user that is nearby.

5. Select one of the people you know has a nearby device that is available for AirDrop just above the row of share options. Their profile pictures will automatically show up with the AirDrop icon.

Note:

- If you are faced with a situation whereby the person you are transferring an item to does not appear as a nearby AirDrop user, you will need to instruct get their Control Center opened on the iPad 8 Gen, iPod touch or iPad 8 Gen from which they can allow AirDrop to start receiving items.

- If you are sending to someone making use of Mac, instruct them to allow themselves to be discoverable in the AirDrop in the Finder.

- If you are sending an item to another option apart from the AirDrop, select the option from the sharing options row which varies depending on the app. In some cases, Siri may suggest ways to share items with people you know by getting their profile pictures and icons displayed representing the sharing methods such as Mail or Messages.

- Lastly, you can also make use of the AirDrop in sharing app and website passwords securely with someone that uses the iPad 8 Gen, iPod touch, iPad 8 Gen or a Mac.

Allowing others to send items from your iPad 8 Gen using AirDrop

1. Go to the Control Center.

2. Tap on the AirDrop icon.

3. Touch and hold the top left groups of controls if the AirDrop icon doesn't show up.

4. Select "Contacts Only" or "Everyone" to select who you like to receive items from.

Note that you have the option of accepting or declining requests as they arrive.

Quit and Restart an iPad 8 Gen App

You can quit an app and get it reopened if you notice it is not working properly. By getting to restart the said app, the problem will get resolved. To do this, you are required to take the following steps:

1. The first step is to quit the app
2. Open the App Switcher.
3. Search for the app by swiping to the right.
4. Swipe up on the app.
5. The second step is to get the app restarted
6. Go to the Home screen.

7. Select the preferred app.Note that if restarting the app does not solve the problem, get the iPad 8 Gen restarted.

Chapter 10: Finding and Buying Books From Apple Books On iPad 8 Gen

Books and audiobooks can be found and purchased directly with the use of the Books app from the Apple Books as well as getting to read and listen to the books immediately from the app.

1. Open books.

2. Tap on the Book Store or Audiobooks to browse titles or select Search to look for a particular title.

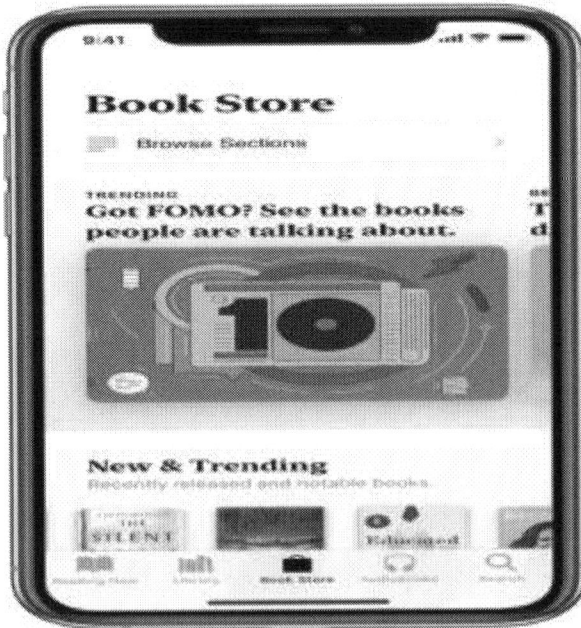

3. Tap on the Book cover to access more details about the book, read or listen to a book sample or get a book added to you "want to read" collection.

4. Select the Buy option to get a title purchased or select the Get option to download a free title.

Note that all purchases are made using a payment method that is associated with your Apple ID.

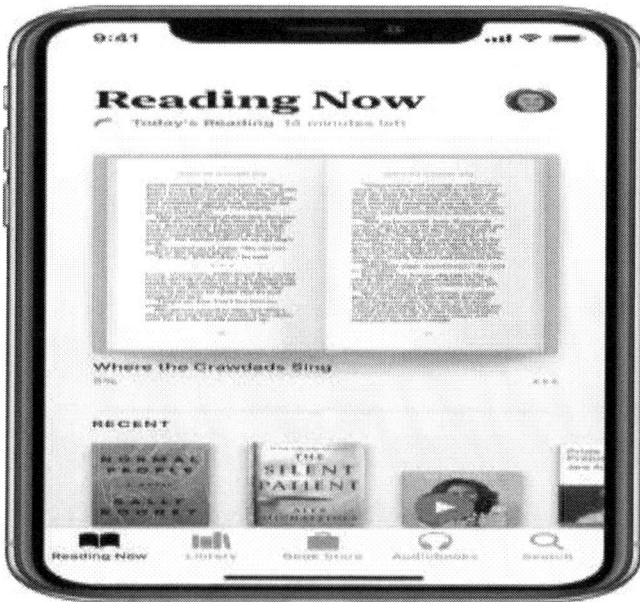

Read books in the Books app on iPad 8 Gen

The Reading Now and Library tabs available in the Books app at the bottom of the screen can be used to view books you are currently reading. You will also have access to get personalized recommendations, learn more about new releases and keep track of books you would like to read.

- Reading now: This feature enables you to access the last book or audiobook you are reading as well as seeing items that were added to your "Want To Read" list including recommendations that are based on the books you purchased.
- Library: With this feature, you will access all books, audiobooks, PDFs, and series you must have gotten from the Book Store including the books you manually added to your library.

Read a Book

1. Select the Reading now or Library tab.
2. Tap a cover to get a book opened.
3. Make use of the following gestures and controls to navigate as follows:

- Turn the page: To do this, tap on the right side of the current page or simply swipe to the left.
- Go back to the previous page: To do this, tap on the left side of the page or simply swipe left to the right.
- Go to a specific page: The first thing to do here is to tap on the page and then move the slider located at the bottom of the screen to the left or right side. Alternatively, you can

tap the search button and enter a page number after which you tap on the page number available in the search results.

- Close a book: To show the controls, tap on the center of the page and tap the Back button afterward.

Changing Text and Display Appearance

1. Tap on the page.
2. Select the Appearance button.
3. Then, you can carry out any of the following actions:

- Adjusting the screen brightness: Do this by dragging the slider to the right or left side.

- Changing the font-size: Increase the font size by tapping on the large A and decrease the font size by tapping on the small size A.

- Change the font: Select Fonts to choose from different font available.

- Changing the page background color: To do this, tap on a colored circle.

- Dimming the screen when it is dark: Turning on the Auto-Night Theme will automatically change the page color and brightness if you are using Books in low-light conditions. Note that not all books will support the Auto-Night theme.

- Turn off pagination: To scroll through a book continuously, turn the Scrolling View on.

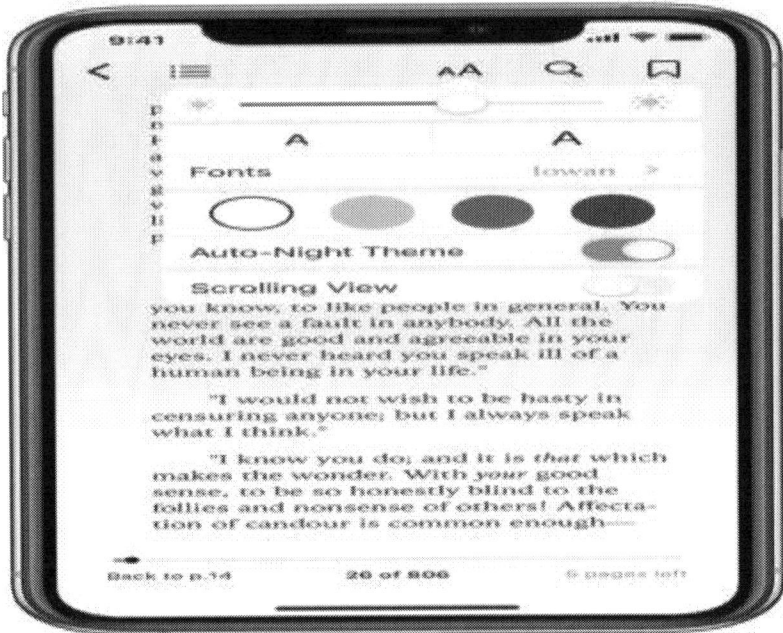

Bookmark a Page

Once a book is closed, your place will be saved automatically and you will not have to get a bookmark added. However, it is advisable to get pages you would like to return to again bookmarked.

1. To add a bookmark, tap the Bookmark Ribbon.
2. To remove a bookmark, tap the Bookmark Ribbon again.
3. To view all your bookmarks:
4. Select the Table of Contents button.
5. Tap Bookmarks.

Highlight or Underline Text

1. Touch and hold the word.
2. To adjust the selection, move the grab points.
3. Tap on Highlight
4. Select the Highlight Color Chooser button to choose your preferred highlight color or to underline.

Removing a Highlight or Underline:

1. Tap the text.
2. Select the Trash button.

To view all your highlights:

1. Tap the Table of contents button.
2. Select Notes

Adding a Note

1. Touch and hold the word.
2. To adjust the selection, move the grab points.

Select Note

1. Enter your texts using the keyboard.
2. Select Done

To access all your notes, take the following steps:

1. Tap the Table of contents button.

2. Select Notes.

3. To get a note deleted, swipe left on the note.

Share a Selection

- Text selections can be sent making use of AirDrop, Messages or Mail. Alternatively, you can send the text selection by adding it to Notes.

- A link to the book will be included in the selection of the book's source which is from the Book Store.

- It is important to note that sharing may not be available for all regions.

To share a selection, you are required to take the following steps:

1. Touch and hold the word.

2. To adjust the selection, move the grab points.

3. Select Share

4. Select a method.

A link can also be sent to view the book in the Bookstore by:

1. Tap on any page.

2. Tap the Table of Contents button.

3. Select the Share button.

Access Your Books on All Devices

Your Book's information can be kept updated across all your devices as long as you have the same Apple ID signed in on them.

Reading Now and Library

1. Go to Settings.
2. Select [your name].
3. Click on "iCloud."
4. Turn both the iCloud Drive and Books on.
5. Then go to Settings
6. Select Books
7. Turn Reading Now on.

Reading position, notes, and highlights

1. Go to Settings.
2. Select [your name].
3. Click on "iCloud."
4. Turn both the iCloud Drive and Books on.

Listening to Audiobooks in Books on iPad 8 Gen

Books apps can be used in listening to audiobooks on your iPad 8 Gen.

How to Play An Audiobook

1. Go to your Library.
2. Select Reading now or Audiobooks collection.

3. Tap the audiobook cover.

4. Then you can perform the following actions:

• Skip forward or backward: To do this, touch and hold the rounded arrows or slide and hold the book covers. To get the number of seconds it takes skipping advances to change, go into the Settings and select the Books option.

• Speeding it up or slowing it down: Go to the lower-left corner and tap on the playback speed to select your preferred speed.

For example, selecting 1x provides you with a normal speed, 0.75x provides three-quarters speed, etc.

• Set a sleep timer: To do this, tap on the Sleep button and select duration afterward.

• Go to a chapter: To navigate to a particular chapter, tap on the Table of Contents button and select a chapter afterward. You should, however, note that some audiobooks do refer chapters as tracks.

• Go to a specific time: Get the playhead dragged directly below the audiobook cover. A gray circle is used to mark the point where you started listening to the audiobook on the timeline. To go back to that spot, simply tap the Circle.

How to set reading goals in Books on iPad 8 Gen

• With the Book apps, you can track how many minutes you read every day including how many books and audiobooks you get done with each year.

• The goals can be customized such that you spend more time reading, setting new reading streaks and getting to share your achievements with your loved ones.

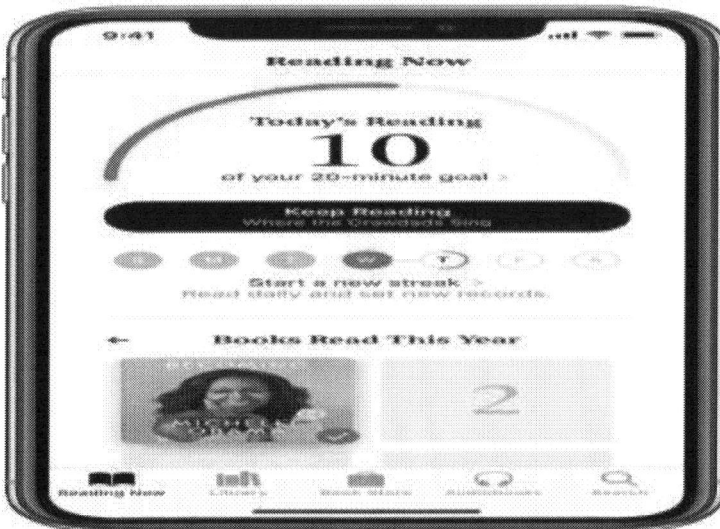

How to Change Your Daily Reading Goal

• Your daily reading goal can be adjusted based on how many minutes you intend to read per day. It is to be noted that this is set to five minutes per day by default if you are yet to customize your daily reading goal.

• To change your daily reading goal, take the following steps:

1. Tap on the Reading Now tab.

2. Swipe down to Reading Goals.

3. Select the Reading counter.

4. Tap Adjust Goal.

5. Set the minutes per day.

6. Tap Done.

Once you have reached your daily reading goal limit, you will be prompted with a notification from Books. Tap on it to get more details regarding your achievement and also get to share your achievements with your loved ones.

How to Change Your Yearly Reading Goal

• Once you are done reading a book or audiobook in the Books app, the **Books Read This Year collection** will be displayed below Reading Goals.

• By default, the yearly reading goal is set to three books per year but this can be altered to your preferred goal depending on how many books you intend to finish. To do this, you are required to take the following steps:

1, Tap the Reading Now tab.

2. Swipe down to Books Read This Year.

2. Tap a gray placeholder square or book cover.

4. Select Adjust Goal.

5. Set the number of books you want to read per year.

5. Tap Done.

Once your yearly reading goal is reached, you will be prompted with a notification from Books. Tap on this to get more details regarding your achievement and get to share with your loved ones.

Seeing Your Reading Streaks and Records

• You can get to find out how many days in a row you were able to reach your daily reading goal from the Books app. It also gets you notified when you set a record.

• Tap "Reading Now" and swipe down to "Reading Goals" to view your current reading streak and record.

How to Turn Off Notifications and Reading Goals

Turn off notifications: To stop getting notifications whenever you achieve a reading goal or a reading streak is set, you are required to take the following steps:

1. Go to the top-right corner of the Reading Now tab.

2. Tap your account.

3. Select Notifications.

4. Turn off "Reading Goals"

Turn off Reading Goals:

1. Go to Settings.

2. Tap on Books.

3. Turn off "Reading Goals"

The reading indicators available in the Reading Now will now be hidden and notifications will be turned off as well.

Organizing Books in the Books App on iPad 8 Gen

The books and audiobooks that are purchased by you are saved in your library in the Books app and they are automatically sorted into collections such as Audiobooks, Want to Read and Finished.

Creating a Collection and Adding Books to It

To get your collections created to personalize your library, you are required to take the following steps:

1. Tap Library.

2. Tap Collections.

3. Select New Collection.

4. Name the collection such as Book Club or Beach Reads.

5. Tap Done.

To add a book to the collection, you are required to take the following steps:

1. Scroll below the book cover.

2. Tap the More Info button (Alternatively, tap on the book's details page available in the Book Store).

3. Tap Add to Collection.

4. Choose your preferred collection.

Note that you have the option to get the same book added to multiple collections.

Sorting Books in Your Library

1. Tap Library.

2. Tap Sort.

3. Choose Recent, Author, Title, Auto or Manually.

4. Tap the Table of Contents button to see books by their title or cover.

Removing Books, Audiobooks, and PDFs

Books, audiobooks, and PDFs can be removed from Reading Now as well as your library collections or get them hidden on your iPad 8 Gen by taking the following steps:

1. Tap Library.

2. Select Edit.

3. Select the items you want to remove.

4. Tap the Trash button.

5. Choose an option.

To unhide the books you must have hidden, you are required to take the following steps:

1. Tap Reading Now.

2. Tap on your account icon.

3. Select Manage Hidden Purchases.

Reading PDF documents in Books on iPad 8 Gen

PDFs that have been received through the Mail, Messages as well as other apps can be opened and saved in the Books app.

Opening PDFs in Books

To do this, you can follow one of the two sets of instructions:

1. Touch and hold the PDF attachment.

2. Select Copy to Books.

OR

1. Tap on the PDF attachment to open it.

2. Select the Share button.

3. Tap Copy to Books.

Emailing or Printing a PDF document

1. Open the PDF document.

2. Tap on the Share button.

3. Select Mail or Print.

Mark up PDF

1. Open the PDF document.

2. Tap the Markup button to make use of the drawing and annotation tools.

Note: If you can't see the Markup button, tap near the center of a page.

Viewing PDFs across Devices

PDFs and books that are not from the Book store can be viewed across your iPad 8 Gen, iPod touch, iPad 8 Gen and Mac as long as you are signed in with your Apple ID.

1. Go to Settings.
2. Select [your name].
3. Tap on iCloud.
4. Turn on iCloud Drive.
5. Turn on Books.
6. Then, go to Settings.
7. Select Books.
8. Turn on iCloud Drive.

Using Calculator on iPad 8 Gen

Basic arithmetic calculations can be performed in the Calculator app for the iPad 8 Gen using the standard calculator. The scientific calculator is also made available for exponential, trigonometric and logarithmic functions.

- To make use of the scientific calculator, get it rotated to the landscape orientation.

Copy, Delete or Clear Numbers

Copy a calculation result:

1. Touch and hold the calculation result on the display.

2. Select Copy.

3. Paste the result in a different location such as the message or note.

Delete the last digit: If a mistake is made while entering a number, delete by simply swiping to the left or right on the display at the top.

Clear the display: Select the Clear (C) key to get the last entry deleted or Select the All Clear (AC) key to get all entries deleted.

Chapter 11: Take Photos with the Camera on iPad 8 Gen

You can make use of the iPad 8 Gen camera and take great photos by choosing from the available camera modes such as Photo, Pano, Video, Slo-mo, Time-lapse, and Portrait. You can also get to enhance your photos using camera features such as Night mode, filters, Live Photos, and Burst.

Taking A Photo

- When your camera is initially opened, the standard mode that you are prompted with is the Photo.
- You can make use of this photo mode to take still photos.
- However, you can swipe to the left or right if you decide to choose a different mode such as Video, Pano, Slo-mo, Time-lapse, and Portrait.

1. Tap in the Home screen or swipe to the left from the Lock screen to open the camera in Photo mode.
2. Tap the Shutter button or press any of the volume buttons to have a shot taken.

To turn flash on or off:

1. Tap the Flash button.
2. Select Auto, On or Off.

You can also set a timer, get your shot framed and stabilize your iPad 8 Gen.

1. Tap the Camera Controls button.

2. Tap the Timer button..

Zoom in or out

1. Open Camera.

2. Zoom in or out by pinching the screen.

Alternatively,

1. Zoom in by toggling between the 1x Zoom button or the 2x Zoom button.

2. Zoom beyond 2x by touching and holding the zoom control, after which you will get the slider dragged to the left.

Or

1. Zoom in by toggling between the 1x Zoom button or the 2x Zoom button.

2. Zoom out by toggling between the .5 Zoom buttons.

3. Zoom beyond 2x by touching and holding the zoom control and then dragging the slider to the left.

Adjust The Camera's Focus and Exposure

- The iPad 8 Gen camera has been designed to automatically set the focus and exposure before taking a photo with the face detection balancing the exposure.

- Adjust the focus and exposure manually by:

1. Tap the screen for the automatic focus area and exposure setting to come up.

2. Tapping the location you like to move the focus area.

3. Drag the adjust exposure button up or down next to the focus area to get the exposure adjusted.

Using Night Mode in Low-Light Situations

The Night mode comes in handy in capturing more detail as well as getting your shots brightened in low light situations.

1. In extremely low light situations, the camera is designed to automatically turn on the Night mode. You can manually get the Night mode turned on by tapping on the Night mode button as soon as it appears in other low-light situations.

2. There is a slider that is displayed below the frame which also displayed the Auto recommended time. Apply more time by dragging the slider to Max.

3. Select the Shutter button and hold the camera still as the timer counts down to zero.

Taking a Live Photo

The Live photo is designed to capture whatever happens before and after a picture is taken as well as the audio.

1. Select Photo mode.

2. Turn Live Photos on or off by tapping the Live Photo.

3. Tap on the Shutter button to take a shot.

Note that Live Photos can be edited in Photos. The Live Photos are marked as "Live" in the corner for your albums.

Taking a Selfie

The front-facing camera can be used for taking a selfie in the Photo mode or Portrait mode.

1. You can switch to the front-facing camera by tapping the camera chooser back-facing button.

2. Position your iPad 8 Gen such that it faces you.

3. Tap the arrows inside the frame to increase the field of view and get more captured inside the frame.

4. To take a shot, tap on the Shutter button or press either of the volume buttons.

Taking a Panorama Photo

The Pano mode is used in capturing landscapes or taking other shots that have difficulty in fitting on your camera screen.

1. Select the Pano mode.

2. Tap the Shutter button.

3. Slowly pan in the direction of the arrow while maintaining the centerline.

4. Tap on the Shutter button again and you are done.

Taking a Photo With A Filter

1. Choose Photo or Portrait mode.

2. Tap the Filter button.

3. Select the Camera controls button and tap on the Filter button.

214

4. Swipe the filters to the left or right below the viewer to preview them and select the one you prefer by tapping it.

Taking Bursts Shots

The Bursts mode allows you to take multiple high-speed photos thereby giving you different options to choose from. The Burst Photos can be taken with the rear or front-facing cameras.

1. The Shutter button should be swept to the left to take rapid-fire photos

2. The number of shots taken can be seen in the counter.

3. Stop the burst shots by releasing your finger.

4. Tap on the Burst thumbnail to choose the photos you like to keep. The gray dots below the thumbnail mark helps in suggesting the photos to keep.

5. Tap "Select"

6. For each photo you like to keep, tap the circle in the lower right corner.

7. Tap Done.

Delete all the Burst shots by tapping on the thumbnail and then select the Delete button.

Play and customize a slideshow

A slideshow is a collection of your photos, formatted and set to music.

1. Tap the Photos tab.

2. View photos by All Photos or Days, then tap Select.

3. Tap each photo you want to include in the slideshow, then tap the Share button.

4. From the list of options, tap Slideshow.

5. Tap the screen, then tap Options in the bottom right to change the slideshow theme, music, and more.

Edit photos and videos on iPad 8 Gen

Use the tools in the Photos app to edit photos and videos on your iPad 8 Gen. When you use iCloud Photos, any edits you make are saved across all your devices.

Edit a photo or video

1. In Photos, tap a photo or video thumbnail to view it in full screen.

2. Tap Edit, then swipe left under the photo to view the editing buttons for each effect such as Exposure, Brilliance, and Highlights.

3. Tap a button, then drag the slider to adjust the effect.

The level of adjustment you make for each effect is displayed by the outline around the button, so you can see at a glance which effects have been increased or decreased.

4. To review the effect, tap the effect button to see the shot before and after the effect was applied (or tap the photo to toggle between the edited version and the original).

5. Tap Done to save your edits, or if you don't like your changes, tap Cancel, then tap Discard Changes.

Tip: Tap the Enhance button to automatically adjust the intensity levels of your photo.

Crop, Rotate, or Flip A Photo

1. In Photos, tap a photo or video thumbnail to view it in full screen.

2. Tap Edit, then do any of the following:

- Crop manually: Drag the rectangle corners to enclose the area you want to keep in the photo, or you can pinch the photo open or closed.
- Crop to a standard preset ratio: Tap the Standard Crop button, then choose a ratio like Square, 2:3, 8:10, and more.
- Rotate: Tap the Rotate button to rotate the photo 90 degrees.
- Flip: Tap the Flip button to flip the image horizontally.

2. Tap Done to save your edits, or if you don't like your changes, tap Cancel, then tap Discard Changes.

Straighten and Adjust Perspective

1. In Photos, tap a photo or video thumbnail to view it in full screen

2. Tap Edit, tap the icon, then select an effect button to straighten or adjust the vertical or horizontal perspective.

3. Drag the slider to adjust the effect.

The level of adjustment you make for each effect is displayed by the yellow outline around the button, so you can see at a glance which effects have been increased or decreased. Tap the button to toggle between the edited effect and the original.

Drag to tilt or straighten.

4. Tap Done to save your edits.

Note: Area captured outside of the camera frame can be used to automatically adjust perspective and alignment. A blue Auto icon appears above the photo when an automatic adjustment is applied.

Apply Filter Effects

1. In Photos, tap a photo or video thumbnail to view it in full screen.

2. Tap Edit, then tap to apply filter effects such as Vivid, Dramatic, or Silvertone.

3. Tap a filter, then drag the slider to adjust the effect.

4. To compare the edited photo to the original, tap the photo.

5. Tap Done to save your edits, or if you don't like your changes, tap Cancel, then tap Discard Changes.

Revert an Edited Photo

After you edit a photo and save your changes, you can revert to the original image.

1. Open the edited image, tap Edit, then tap Revert.

2. Tap Revert to Original.

Mark up a photo

1. Tap a photo to view it in full screen.

2. Tap Edit, then tap the more button.

3. Tap Markup .

4. Annotate the photo using the different drawing tools and colors. Tap the Add button to add shapes, text, or even your signature.

Taking Videos with iPad 8 Gen Camera

The camera can be used in recording videos on your iPad 8 Gen which also provides you with the option of changing modes to take slow-mo as well as time-lapse videos.

Recording a video

1. Select Video mode.

2. Select the Record button or tap the volume button to start your recording.

3. In the process of recording, you can perform any of the following actions:

- Snap a still photo by pressing the white Shutter button.

- Zoom in and out by pinching the screen. Zoom in by touching and holding the 1x Zoom button and drag the slider to the left afterward.

- Zoom out by tapping the .5x Zoom button.

4. Stop recording by tapping the Record button or pressing either volume button.

NOTE:

The video records at 30fps by default. You can select other frame rates and video resolution depending on your model by going through the following steps:

1. Go to Settings.

2. Select the Camera.

3. Tap on Record Video.

The more the speed of the frame rate, the higher the resolution and then the larger the video file that is produced.

Turn off the stereo recording by taking the following steps:

1. Go to Settings.

2. Tap on Camera.

3. Turn off Record Stereo Sound.

Recording a Quicktake Video

The QuickTake video can be recorded in the Photo mode. In the process of taking a QuickTake video, the Record button can be moved into the lock position thereby allowing you to take still photos more easily as well as adjusting your shot while recording.

1. Select the Photo mode.

2. Start recording a QuickTake video by touching and holding the Shutter button.

3. Slide Shutter button to the right and release it over the lock of the hands-free recording.

4. To take a still photo while recording a QuickTake video, tap on the Shutter button.

5. Stop recording by tapping on the Record button.

Note: View the QuickTake video in the Photos app by tapping the thumbnail. When the camera automatically gets an adjustment applied to improve the video composition, a blue Auto badge shows up at the top right corner.

Recording a Slow-Motion Video

In the process of recording a slow-motion video, the video will record as normal enabling you to see the slow-mo effect when the video is played back. Video can also be edited such that the slow-mo action start and stop at a particular time chosen by you.

1. Select the Slow-mo mode.

2. To start and stop recording, tap on the Record button or press either of the volume buttons.

- Snap a still photo while recording by tapping the white Shutter button.

- Tap the video thumbnail and then select Edit, select a portion of the video to be played in slow motion while the rest will be played at a regular speed.

- Select the camera chooser back-facing button to record the slow-motion using the front-facing camera.

- The frame rate and resolution can be changed depending on your model.

- If the need arises for you to change the Slo-mo recording settings, you are required to take the following steps:

1. Go to Settings.

2. Select the Camera.

3. Select the Record Slow-mo option.

Capture a Time-Lapse Video

Footage can be captured at selected intervals to create a time-lapse video over some time. To do this, you are required to take the following steps:

1. Select Time-lapse mode.

2. Position your iPad 8 Gen where you like to capture a scene in motion.

3. Start recording by tapping on the Record button.

4. Stop recording by tapping on the Record button again.

Toggle between the 1x zoom button and 2x zoom button to zoom in while for New iPad 8 Gen, zoom out by toggling the 0.5x zoom button.

Trim A Video

1. In Photos, open the video, then tap Edit.

2. Drag either end of the frame viewer, then tap Done.

To undo the trim, tap Edit, then tap Revert.

Take Portrait Mode Photos Using Your iPad 8 Gen Camera

You can apply a depth-of-field effect. It helps in keeping your subject sharp while creating a beautifully blurred background.

Different lighting effects can be applied and adjusted to your Portrait mode photos.

With a TrueDepth camera, a selfie can be taken in the portrait mode.

Taking a Photo in Portrait Mode

Studio-quality lighting effects can be applied to your Portrait mode photos on models that support Portrait lighting.

Choose Portrait mode.

1. Follow the onscreen tips to get your subject framed in the yellow portrait box.

2. Choose a lighting effect by dragging the Portrait Lighting control. You can choose from the following lighting effects:

- Natural Light: This gives the face a sharp focus against a blurred background.

- Studio Light: This brightly lit the face and also gives the photo an overall clean look.

- Contour Light: This gives the face dramatic shadows with highlights and lowlights.

- Stage Light: The face gets spotlit against a deep black background.

- Stage Light Mono: This provides an effect that is similar when compared to the stage light. The only difference is that the photo will be in classic black and white.

- High-Key Light Mono: This feature provides a grayscale subject on a white background.

3. Take a shot by tapping on the Shutter button.

NOTE:

- The stage light, stage light mono, and high-key light mono are only available when making use of the front-facing TrueDepth camera.

- You can remove the Portrait mode effect in Photos after taking a photo in the Portrait mode. To do this, you are required to take the following steps:

1. Open the photo.

2. Select Edit.

3. Tap the Portrait to turn the effect on or off.

Adjust Portrait Lighting Effects in Portrait Mode

The position and intensity of each Portrait Lighting effect can be virtually adjusted to sharpen eyes or get facial features brightened and smooth.

1. Choose Portrait mode.
2. Frame your subject.
3. Go to the top of the screen and tap the Portrait Control button. The Portrait Lighting slider is displayed below the frame.
4. Adjust the effect by dragging the slider to the right or left.
5. Take a shot by tapping the Shutter button.

Once you have taken a photo in the portrait mode, you can adjust the lighting effect further by making use of the Portrait Lighting slider in photos. To do this, open the Portrait mode photo and select Edit.

Adjust Depth Control in Portrait Mode

For Depth Control, make use of the Depth Control slider in adjusting the level of background blur in your Portrait mode photos.

1. Choose Portrait mode.

2. Frame your subject.

3. Go to the top right corner of the screen.

4. Tap the Depth Adjustment button which displays the Depth Control slider below the frame.

5. Adjust the effect by dragging the slider to the right or left.

6. Take a shot by tapping the Shutter button.

Note that the Depth Control slider in Photos can be used to adjust the background blur effect further after taking a photo in the Portrait mode. To do this, open the Portrait mode photo and select Edit.

Capture Content outside the Camera Frame On iPad 8 Gen

The photo on the iPad 8 Gen shows and catches images beyond its frame. you can record and snap the content then create edits subsequently in the Photos application. The camera automatically utilizes the materials outside its frame to enhance your pictures as well as your QuickTake clips.

How to Edit Videos and Photos with Content outside the Frame

Once you switch the Capture Content Outside the Frame on the configurations, the material recorded out of the frame will appear when you use the crop, perspective and straighten instruments to edit.

- To take and capture images beyond the camera frame, click Settings > Camera. Switch the Photos Capture Content Outside the Frame, on.
- When recording videos, the Camera captures materials outside the picture automatically. From Settings go to Camera, and switch off Videos Capture Content Outside the Frame.

Note that if you do not make use of the material recorded out of the camera frame for editing, it will be removed automatically in 30 days.

Adjust Composition with Content outside the Frame

The camera utilizes data captured out of the picture to modify and enhance the structure of a picture or a QuickTake video. Upon instant modification, a blue auto logo emerges in the top-right corner.

To switch off instant modifications, navigate to Settings > Camera, then switch off Auto Apply Adjustments.

Use the Camera Settings on iPad 8 Gen

Discover how to utilize your iPad 8 Gen's camera configuration.

Align your shots

To show a matrix on the camera display that can assist you to streamline your pictures, tap Settings > Camera and switch Grid on.

You can modify view alignment in the Photos tool on your device.

Preserve camera settings

You can maintain the last picture settings, filter, illumination, depth and live photo presets that you used, so that they won't be changed when you unlock the next camera.

1. From Settings > Camera > Preserve Settings.

2. Switch on any of the following:

- **Camera Model:** continues on the last camera configurations you used, like Video or Pano.

- **Creative Controls:** restores the lighting, filters, or depth configurations that you used the last time.

230

- **Live Photo:** restores Live Photo presets.

Adjust the Shutter-Sound Volume

Use Ringer and Alerts to either increase or decrease the shutter sounds.

From Settings go to Sounds(Sounds & Haptics on the system that are compatible with the feature). Or you can silent the sound with the Ring/Silent tab. (some places have muting automatically disabled)

HDR Camera on iPad 8 Gen

Cameras with High Dynamic Range(HDR) enables you to get excellent pictures in the case of increased contrast. iPad 8 Gens capture pictures in fast sequence at distinct exposures and combines them to give your pictures more depth and shade.

By standard, when it is most efficient, the iPad 8 Gen utilizes HDR (for the back camera and front-facing camera).

So, you will have to keep your iPad 8 Gen constant and prevent movement for the finest shots.

Turn Off Automatic HDR

When it is most efficient, the iPad 8 Gen automatically uses the HDR. And you can also operate the function by doing the following:

- On your iPad 8 Gen from Settings go to Camera, then switch Smart HDR off.
- If you want to switch the HDR on from your iPad 8 Gen cameras screen, click HDR, then click on On.
- On your iPad 8 Gen click Settings > Camera, switch Auto HDR off.

If you want your HDR feature back on, press HDR, and then click on from the camera screen.

Keep Only the HDR Version of a Photo

The HDR variant of a picture is stored in Photos automatically. However, both HDR and non-HDR variants can be saved as well.

From Settings go to Camera, and switch the Keep Normal Photo off.

Hint: In Your photo albums, HDR variants are labeled in the corner with "HDR."

View, share, and print photos on the iPad 8 Gen

All videos and pictures you snap with your iPad 8 Gen will be stored in Photos. With the iCloud Photos On in all your gadgets built with the iCloud Photos (versions iOS 8.1 or later or the iPad 8 GenOS 13), all your fresh videos and pictures are uploaded in Photos by default.

Hint; If your Location is on in configuration, go to Privacy. Videos and pictures will have your location data attached to them. This could be utilized by apps and websites that support photo-sharing.

View your photos

1. From Camera, click thumbnail picture by the left corner below the screen

2. Scroll right or left to view the recent pictures you took.

3. Click the display to reveal or hide controls

4. Press All Photos to view all your saved videos and pictures.

Share and Print Your Photos

1. Click the Share tab when looking at your pictures.

2. Choose an option like AirDrop, Messages, Mail, or Print. in some cases you may have to flick to the left at the bottom to show Print

Upload and Sync Photos across Devices

You can Use iCloud Photos to send your videos and pictures to iCloud and examine them with the same Apple ID on your Apple devices. To turn on iCloud Photos, go to Settings then click Photos. Once the iCloud Photos feature is switched off, you can still gather up about a thousand of your latest pictures in **My Photo Stream album,** with gadgets that support iCloud.

Scan a QR code with the iPad 8 Gen camera

For links to webpages, apps, coupon codes, tickets et.c, you can scan Quick Response (QR) codes with your iPad 8 Gen camera as it can detect and outline codes.

Use the Camera to Read A QR Code

1. Open the Camera, then place the iPad 8 Gen correctly to display the code on the screen.

2. Click on the notice on the screen to go to the webpage or app in question.

Open the QR code reader from Control Center

1. From Settings go to Control Center > Customize Controls, and press the Insert tab beside the QR Code Reader.

2. From the Control Center, click QR code reader, and place your iPad 8 Gen properly to have your code displayed on the screen.

3. For more lighting, click on the flashlight.

Chapter 12: Create and Edit Events in Calendar On iPad 8 Gen

The calendar can be used to get events, appointments and meetings created and edited. Siri can be asked to say something like:

"Do I have a meeting at 12?"

"Where is my 5 pm meeting?"

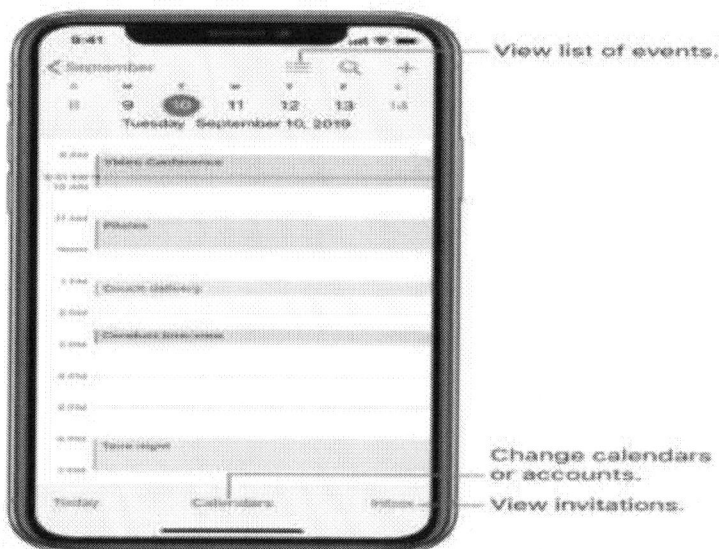

Adding an event

1. Go to the top right.

2. Select the Add button.

3. Input the event details.

The event details should include the title and event location, start and end times, how often an event repeats, etc.

Add an alert

The alert feature can be set such that it reminds you of when an event beforehand. To add an alert you are required to take the following steps:

1. Tap the event.
2. Go to the top right.
3. Select Edit.
4. Go to the event details.
5. Tap Alert.
6. Select when to be reminded such as 5 minutes before the event, at the time of the event, etc.

NOTE: It is to be noted that if the event's location has been added when filling in the event details, the calendar makes use of the Apple Maps to search for information such as the location, traffic conditions including transit option to notify you of when to leave for the event.

Adding an Attachment

You can add an attachment to a Calendar event and share with invitees. To add an attachment, you want take the following steps:

1. Tap the Event.
2. Go to the top right.
3. Select Edit.
4. Go to the event details.
5. Select Add attachment.

6. The File opens showing files that were recently opened.

7. Find the file you want to attach. Do this by scrolling, tap folders to get them opened, tap Browse to look in other locations like the iCloud Drive, enter the filename in the search field, etc.

8. Tap Done.

To remove the attachment, you are required to take the following steps:

1. Tap the Event.

2. Go to the top right.

3. Select Edit.

4. Swipe left over the attachment.

5. Tap Remove.

Finding Events in Other Apps

Events found in Messages, Mail, and safari can be suggested by Siri so that they can be easily added to the Calendar app. These events may include flight reservations, hotel bookings, etc.

1. Go to Settings.

2. Select Calendar.

3. Select Siri & Search.

4. Turn on Show Siri Suggestions in App to enable Siri in suggesting events available in other apps.

NOTE: Turn on Learn from this App to enable Siri in making suggestions in other apps based on how you use your Calendar.

Editing an Event

The time of events, as well as any other details, can be changed at any time.

Change the time:

1. Touch and hold the event in a day view.
2. Drag it to a new time or simply adjust the grab points.

Change Event Details:

1. Tap the Event.
2. Go to the top right.
3. Select Edit.
4. Go to the event details.
5. Select a setting to change it or tap into a field to enter new information.

Deleting an Event

1. In the day view, select the event.
2. Go to the bottom of the screen.
3. Tap Delete Event.

Sending and Receiving Invitations In Calendar On iPad 8 Gen

- You can send and receive meeting and event invitations using the Calendar app.

- With the Microsoft Exchange, iCloud and some CalDAV servers, you can get to send and receive meetings' invitation.

- It is, however, important to note that not every feature is supported by all calendar servers.

Inviting Others to an Event

1. Tap the event.
2. Select Edit.
3. Tap Invitees.
4. Tap Add Invitees.
5. Input in the names or email addresses of invitees or tap the Add button to select Contacts.
6. Tap Done or simply select Send if the event was not scheduled.

OR if the event was not scheduled, you can take the following steps alternatively:

1. Tap the event.
2. Tap Invitees.
3. Select the Send Mail to Invitees button.
4. Input in the names or email addresses of invitees or tap the Add button to select Contacts.
5. Tap Done or simply select Send if the event was not scheduled.

NOTE: People can be invited to anvevent even if it was not scheduled by you with Microsoft Exchange and other servers.

If you want to turn off notifications when someone declines a meeting, you are required to take the following steps:

1. Go to Settings.

2. Select Calendar.

3. Turn off Show Invitee Declines.

Replying To an Event Invitation

1. To reply to event notification, tap it or go to the Calendar app, select Inbox and tap an invitation.

2, Select your response from the available options which include Accept, Maybe, or Decline.

For an invitation which was received by email, to respond:

3. Tap on the underlined text in the email.

4. Tap Show in Calendar.

NOTE:

- In case you have added comments to your response, note that comments are not available for all calendars app.

- Your comments will, however, be visible to the organizer but not the attendees.

- To view the events that you must have declined, take the following steps:

1. Go to the bottom of the screen.

2. Tap Calendars.

3. Turn on Show Declined Events.

Schedule an Event without Blocking Your Schedule

An event can be added to your calendar without the timeframe showing up busy to others who sent you invitations.

1. Tap the event.
2. Select Edit.
3. Tap Show as.
4. Tap Free.

Suggest a Different Meeting Time

Different meeting times can be suggested for a meeting invitation received by you. To do this you are required to take the following steps:

1. Tap the meeting.
2. Select Propose New Time.
3. Tap the time.
4. Input a new time.

Note: The organizer will receive either a counter-proposal or an email having your suggestion depending on the capabilities of your calendar server.

Sending an Email Quickly To Attendees

1. Tap an Event with attendees.
2. Select Invitees.
3. Tap the Send Mail to Invitees button.

Change How Events Are Viewed in Calendar On iPad 8 Gen

You can get to view a day, a week, a month or a year at a time as well as viewing a list of upcoming events in the Calendar app on iPad 8 Gen.

To change the view of the Calendar, you can do any of the following:

Zoom in or out: To zoom in or out on your calendar, tap a year, month or day. In the case of a week or day view, you are required to pinch to zoom in or out.

View a weekly calendar: Rotate the iPad 8 Gen sideways in a day view.

View a list of events: Tap the List button to view the day's events in month view. Tap on the List button again to go back to the month view.

Search for events in Calendar on iPad 8 Gen

You can easily search for events based on their title, location, invitees and notes. To do this:

1. Tap the Search button.
2. Enter the text you want to find in the search field.

You can also ask Siri by saying something like; "What's on my calendar for Thursday?"

Customizing Your Calendar on iPad 8 Gen

You can get to do the following with your Calendar:

- Choose alternate calendars such as displaying Chinese or Hebrew dates.
- Display week numbers.
- Override the automatic time zone.
- Choose the day of the week Calendar starts with.
- And many more

To do all these, you are required to take the following steps:

1. Go to Settings.
2. Select Calendar.
3. Choose your preferred settings and features.

Changing How Calendar Notifies on Your iPad 8 Gen

How you get to receive notification for invitations, events found in apps, upcoming events and many more can be changed by taking the following steps:

1. Go to Settings.
2. Select Notifications.
3. Select Calendar.
4. Turn on Allow Notifications.
5. Select the type of event such as Upcoming Events.
6. Select where you want the notifications for those events to be displayed. For example, the lock screen, as banners at the top of the screen, in the Notification center, using alert sound, etc.

Set Up Multiple Calendars on iPad 8 Gen

- Multiple calendars can be set up in the Calendar app to keep track of different kinds of events. This doesn't mean you can't keep track of all your events and appointments in one Calendar, the choice is yours.

- However, setting up additional calendars helps you to stay organized.

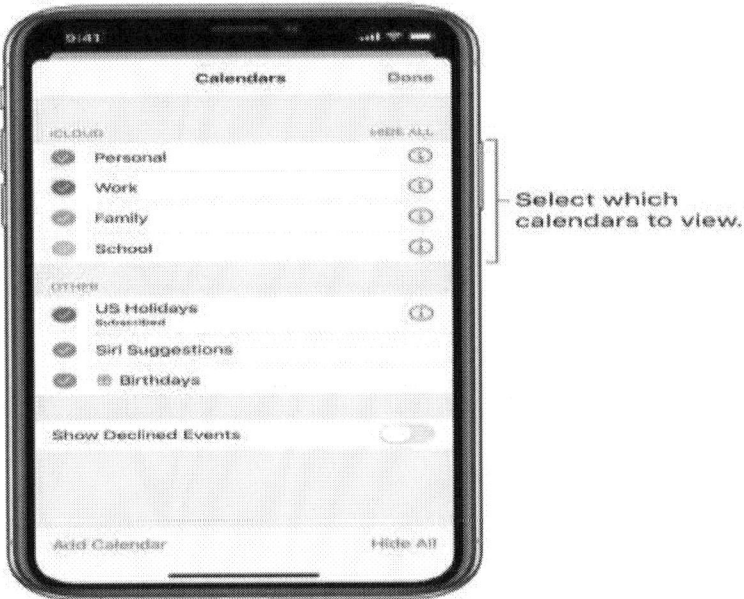

Viewing Multiple Calendars At Once

1. Go to the bottom of the screen.

2. Tap Calendars.

3. Perform any of the following actions:

- Select your preferred calendars.

- Select US holidays such that it includes national holidays with your events.

- Select Birthdays such that it includes birthdays from Contacts with your events.

Setting a Default Calendar

One of your calendars can be made the default calendar. Whenever you add an event with the use of Siri or other apps, it gets automatically added to your default calendar.

1. Go to Settings.
2. Select Calendar.
3. Select the Default Calendar.
4. Choose the calendar you want to make your default calendar.

Changing a Calendar's Color

1. Go to the bottom of the screen.
2. Tap Calendars.
3. Select the Info button next to the calendar.
4. Select a color
5. Tap Done.

Note that for some calendar accounts like Google, the server is responsible for setting the color.

Turn on iCloud, Exchange, Google, or Yahoo calendars

1. Go to Settings.
2. Select Passwords & Accounts.

3. Select Add Account.

4. Select Other.

5. Tap Add CalDAV Account or Add Subscribe Calendar.

6. Input the server information.

Subscribe To a Calendar

1. Go to Settings.

2. Select Passwords & Accounts.

3. Select Add Account.

4. Select Other.

5. Tap Add Subscribe Calendar.

6. Input the URL of the .ics file to subscribe to including any other required server information.

Note: An iCalendar (.ics) calendar can also be subscribed to by tapping a link to the calendar.

Add a Caldav Account

1. Go to Settings.

2. Select Passwords & Accounts.

3. Select Add Account.

4. Select Other.

5. Tap Add CalDAV Account.

6. Input in the server information.

Moving an Event to another Calendar

1. Tap the event.

2. Tap Calendar.

3. Choose a calendar to move the event to.

Sharing iCloud Calendars on iPad 8 Gen

- An iCloud calendar can be shared with other iCloud users in the Calendar app. Others will get to see the calendar shared and you can also allow them to add or change events.

- A read-only version of the calendar can also be shared for anyone to view. If the Family sharing has been set up, a calendar that is shared with all the members of the family will be automatically created.

Create an iCloud Calendar

1. Go to the bottom screen.

2. Tap Calendars.

3. Tap Add Calendar.

4. Input the name of the new calendar.

5. Tap Done.

Share an iCloud Calendar

You can choose who to share your calendar with in iCloud and those that are invited will receive an invitation to join the calendar.

1. Go to the bottom screen.
2. Tap Calendars.
3. Tap on the info button which is next to the iCloud calendar you like to share.
4. Select Add Person.
5. Enter a name or email address or select the Add button to browse your contacts.
6. Tap Add.

Change a Person's Access to a Shared Calendar

After inviting a person to share your calendar, you can prevent them from editing the calendar or stop sharing the calendar with that person.

1. Tap Calendars.
2. Tap on the info button next to the shared calendar.
3. Tap the name of the person.
4. Perform any of the following actions:
- Turn Allow Editing on or off.
- Tap Stop Sharing.

Turn Off Notifications for Shared Calendars

You will be notified of any change that has been made to the calendar you have shared with someone. If you don't want to receive these notifications, you can get it turned off by taking the following steps:

1. Go to Settings.
2. Select Notifications.
3. Tap Calendar.
4. Tap Shared Calendar Changes.
5. Turn off Allow Notifications.

Share a Read-Only Calendar with Anyone

1. Tap Calendars.
2. Tap the info button which is next to the iCloud calendar you want to share.
3. Turn on Public Calendar.
4. Tap the Share Link to copy or send a URL for your calendar.
5. Select a method for sending the URL. Examples of available methods include Mail, Message, etc.

Note that anyone the URL is sent to can make use of it in subscribing to the calendar with the use of a compatible app such as the Calendar for macOS.

Delete a Calendar

1. Go to the bottom screen.

2. Tap Calendars. Tap on the info button which is next to the iCloud calendar you like to delete.

3. At the bottom of the list, Tap Delete Calendar.

Chapter 13: See the Time in Cities Worldwide On iPad 8 Gen

If you want to check on the various time zones from around the globe utilize the Clock application.

Ask Siri. Speak a command like: "What's the time in Liverpool?" or "What says the clock?"

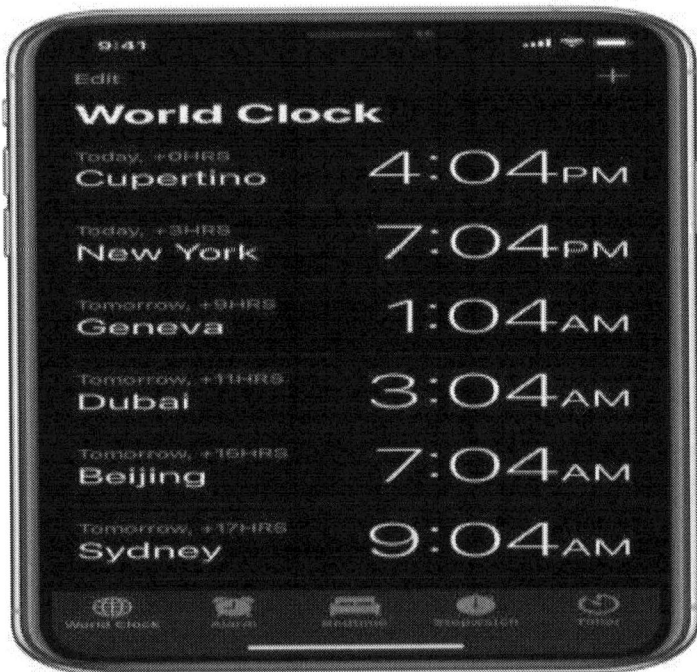

1. Press World Clock.

2. To organize your choice cities, click Edit, and carry out any of the actions below:

- Press the Add tab, and choose a city, to add a place.
- Click on the Delete tab to delete a place.
- Move the Reorder tab up or down to rearrange places.

Set an Alarm or Bedtime Schedule on iPad 8 Gen

You can set up an alarm with the Clock app to either ring or vibrate at a particular moment. You can also create a sleep timetable that tells you when to go to bed and wake up.

Ask Siri: Speak a command like "Remind me about the Party by 6 a.m. every day" or "Fix a 5 p.m. alarm tomorrow."

Set an Alarm

1. Click on Alarm, and press the Add tab.

2. Fix a time, and select whichever actions below:

- Repeat: pick the days.

- Label: You can name the alarm like "wash the dishes."
- Sound: select your ringtone or vibration.
- Snooze: Grant yourself 9 minutes more.

3. Press Save.

If you want to switch or remove your alarm, click Edit.

Set a bedtime schedule

1. Click on Bedtime below the screen and press Set Up, then execute the directions on the display.

2. Click Bedtime and switch on Bedtime Schedule.

Change Your Bedtime Schedule

Execute any of the following to modify your bedtime timetable:

- Specify alarm days: Tap the weekdays.
- Slide the Bedtime and Wake keys to modify your bed and wake periods.
- Switch off reminders for sleep: press the Return key, click Options, click on bedtime reminders then press None.

You can switch the Do Not Disturb on or off during bedtime in Options, monitor your bedtime and change your wake-up tune.

Track Your Sleep History

1. Click Bedtime, then navigate to Analysis showing your latest sleep record.

If you operate your iPad 8 Gen device while sleeping, you're not going to get credit for that moment.

2. Click "Show more in Health" to view your total sleep record in the Health function.

3. Click Add Data in the top-right corner of your Sleep Analysis from the Health app to add details to your sleep records.

Use the timer or stopwatch on iPad 8 Gen

Utilize the timer in the Clock app to count down from a given time. There is also the stopwatch to evaluate an event's length.

Ask Siri. You can speak commands such as: "fix a 5-minute timer" or "Start timer."

Set the Timer

1. Press Timer.

2. Fix the time and sound to be played when the timer is finished. Hint: You can fix the timer to prevent the replay if you intend to fall asleep while playing music or a video. Click when the timer ends and press Stop Playing below the screen.

3. Press Start.

Even when you operate another function or your iPad 8 Gen sleeps, the timer still counts on.

Track time with the stopwatch

1. Click the stopwatch. if you want to change your clock faces from digital to analog flick on the stopwatch screen.

2. Press Start.

Even when you launch another app or if your iPad 8 Gen screen sleeps, the timer is still on.

3. Press on Lap if you want to record either a lap or split timer.

4. Press Stop to end recording.

5. To wipe the stopwatch press Reset.

Use the Compass on iPad 8 Gen

The Compass interface displays to you the position, place, and altitude of your iPad 8 Gen.

See Your Bearings, Coordinates, and Elevation

Below the screen, your bearings, GPS location, and altitude are displayed.

1. Keep your iPad 8 Gen flat to match the crosshairs in the middle of the compass for precise bearings.

2. Click the button of the compass to save your present position. When you're off track, a red band emerges.

Press the positions at the lower edge of the display to display your position in Maps.

Allow Compass to Access Your Location

If the Compass cannot find your position, please ensure that you have activated Location.

1. From Settings go to Privacy > Location Services, and switch Location Services on.

2. Click Compass and press While Utilizing the application.

Important: Magnetic or external disruptions can affect the compass accuracy; also the magnets inside your iPad 8 Gen EarPods can trigger a shift. therefore use the function only to help with fundamental navigation. Do not depend on it to know the exact place, closeness, range or direction.

Share your ETA

As you follow turn-by-turn driving instructions, you can let others know your estimated time of arrival (ETA). (Standard carrier data and text rates may apply.)

1. With turn-by-turn directions showing, tap the route card, then tap Share ETA.

2. Choose one or more suggested contacts, or tap Contacts to find a contact.

3. You can do the following during your trip:

- Cancel sending ETA information: Tap Sharing ETA at the bottom of the screen, then choose a contact.

- Replace the Sharing ETA card with the route card: Tap the Close button on the Sharing ETA card.

People using devices with iOS 13, iPad 8 GenOS 13, or later receive a Maps notification with your ETA, and they can track your progress in Maps. People using devices with iOS 12 or earlier receive the notification through iMessage. People using other mobile devices receive an SMS message.

View turn-by-turn or stop-by-stop directions for walking or transit routes

Ask Siri. Say something like: "Transit directions to my dad's work."

Or you can find a walking or transit route, then tap Go.

As Maps follows your progress, it shows your location on the route. Do any of the following at any time during your trip:

- End directions at any time: Tap End, or say something to Siri like "Stop navigating."
- See the next instruction: Swipe left on the banner at the top of the screen.
- View the directions in a list: Tap the route card at the bottom of the screen, then tap Details.
- See the route overview: Tap the route card at the bottom of the screen, then tap Overview. To see more detail, tap the route card, then tap "Turn-by-turn" (for a walk route) or Zoom In (for a transit route).
- Add a transit stop to Favorites.

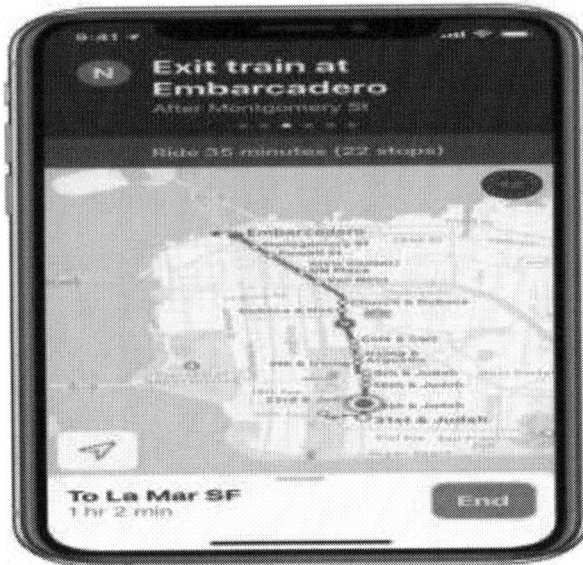

Sign in with Apple on iPad 8 Gen

With Sign in with Apple, you can sign in to participating apps and websites with your Apple ID. By using your Apple ID to set up and sign in to accounts, you don't need to fill out forms or create and remember new passwords.

Sign in with Apple is designed to respect your privacy. Apps and websites can ask only for your name and email address to set up your account, and Apple won't track you as you use them.

Set Up An Account And Sign In

When a participating app or website asks you to set up an account or to sign up for the first time, do the following:

1. Tap Sign in with Apple.

2. Follow the onscreen instructions.

Some apps (and websites) won't request any personal information from you. In this case, you simply authenticate with Face ID or Touch ID (depending on your model), then start using the app.

Others may ask for your name and email address to set up a personalized account. When an app asks for this information, Signing in with Apple displays your name and personal email address from your Apple ID account for you to review.

To edit your name, tap it, then use the keyboard to make changes.

To specify an email address, do one of the following:

• Use your personal email address: Tap Share My Email. If you have multiple email addresses associated with your Apple ID, choose the address you want.

• Hide your email address: Tap Hide My Email.

When you choose this option, Apple creates a unique, anonymized address for you that forwards email from the app to your personal address. This option allows you to receive email from the app without sharing your personal email address.

After you review your information and choose an email option, tap Continue, authenticate with Face ID or Touch ID (depending on your model), then start using the app.

Sign In to Access Your Account

After you set up an account with an app or website using Sign in with Apple, you typically don't need to sign in to it again on your iPad 8 Gen. But if you're asked to sign in (for example, after you sign out of an account), do the following:

1. Tap Sign in with Apple.

2. Review the Apple ID that appears, then tap Continue.

3. Authenticate with Face ID or Touch ID (depending on your model).

Change the Address Used To Forward Email

If you chose to hide your email address when you created an account and you have more than one address associated with your Apple ID, you can change the address that receives your forwarded email.

1. Go to Settings > [your name] > Name, Phone Numbers, Email > Forward To.

2. Choose a different email address, then tap Done.

Change Sign in with Apple settings for an app or website

1. Go to Settings > [your name] > Password and Security.

2. Tap Apps Using Your Apple ID.

3. Choose an app, then do either of the following:

- Turn off forwarding email: Turn off Forward To. You won't receive any further emails from the app.

- Stop using Sign in with Apple: Tap Stop Using Apple ID. You may be asked to create a new account the next time you try to sign in with the app.

Sign in with Apple also works on your other devices—iPad 8 Gen, Apple Watch, Mac, Apple TV, and iPod touch—where you're signed in with the same Apple ID.

To sign in from an Android app, a Windows app, or any web browser, tap Sign in with Apple, then enter your Apple ID and password.

Sign in with Apple requires two-factor authentication for your Apple ID. This protects your Apple ID, your app accounts, and your app content.

Chapter 14: Mark A Device as Lost in Find My On iPad 8 Gen

Make use of the Find My app in marking your missing iPad 8 Gen, iPod touch, iPad 8 Gen, Mac and Apple Watch as lost to prevent intruders from accessing your personal information. To do this, you will need to turn on Find My [device] before you lose it.

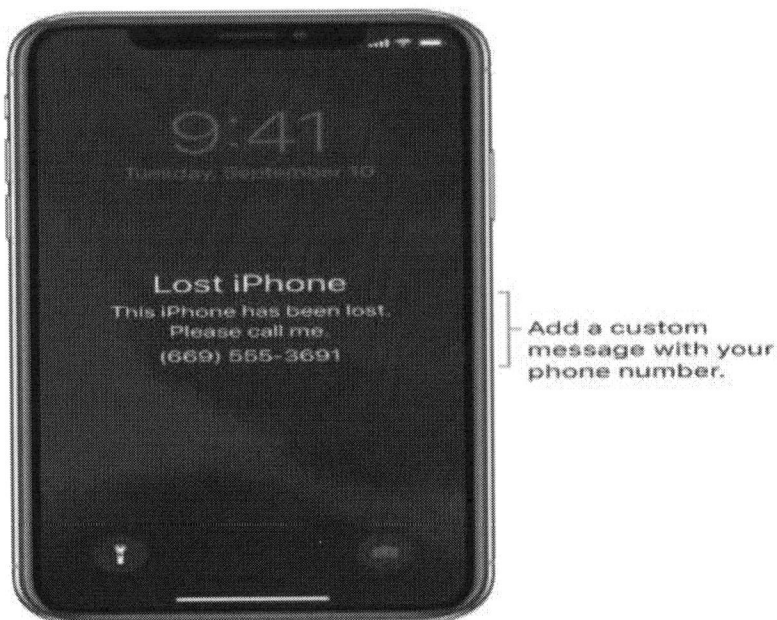

Consequences of Marking Your Device as Lost

• You will receive a confirmation email on your Apple ID email address.

• A custom message can be displayed by you on the screen of your device with which you indicate that the device is lost or how you can be contacted to get it back.

• When a message or notification is received or if an alarm goes off, the device will not display such alerts or make any noise. Nevertheless, it will still be able to receive phone calls as well as FaceTime calls.

• The Apple Pay feature will be disabled for your device. Information on your credit or debit cards that have been set up for Apple Pay including students ID cards and Express Transit cards will be removed from your device. The credit, debit and student cards will be removed even if your device is in the offline mode while the Express Transit cards will wait till your devices go online to be removed as well.

• You will be able to see the current location of your device on the map as well as any change in its location for iPad 8 Gen, iPod touch, iPad 8 Gen or Apple Watch devices.

Mark A Device as Lost

The Lost Mode of your iPad 8 Gen, iPod touch or Apple Watch can be turned on if you have lost your device. Mac can also be locked as well.

Go to the Devices list.

1. Tap the lost device.
2. Tap Activate below "Mark As Lost"
3. You will be prompted with on-screen instructions to follow while also keeping the following in mind.

Passcode: You will need to create a passcode if your iPad 8 Gen, iPod touch, iPad 8 Gen or Apple Watch doesn't have one. For your Mac device, you will need to create a numerical passcode even if there is already a password set up on your Mac.

4. It is to be noted that the passcode is different from your password and it will only be requested when your device is marked as lost.

• **Contact Information**: You need to enter a phone number where you can be reached if you are asked to enter a phone number. If prompted to enter a message, make sure you indicate that the device is lost including where you can be contacted if found. Both the phone number and message will be displayed on the Lock screen.

5. For iPad 8 Gen, iPod touch, iPad 8 Gen or Apple Watch, you will select "Activate" while for Mac, you will select "Lock."

Note: Activated will be tagged below the Mark As Lost section once your device has been marked as lost. In a case where your device wasn't connected to a Wi-Fi or Cellular network when it was marked as lost, it will appear as pending until your device gets online again.

Changing Contact Information or Email Notifications for A Lost Device

Your contact information or email notification settings can be updated even after marking your iPad 8 Gen, iPod touch, iPad 8

Gen or Apple Watch as lost. To do this you are required to take the following steps:

1. Go to the Devices list.

2. Tap the lost device.

3. Tap Pending or Activated below "Mark As Lost"

4. Then perform any of the following action:

• Change contact information: Make changes depending on your preference.

• Get email updates: If not already on, you can turn on Receive Email Updates.

5. Tap Done.

Turn off Lost Mode for an iPad 8 Gen, iPod touch, iPad 8 Gen or Apple Watch

Once you find your lost device, you will need to do any of the following to turn off the Lost Mode:

• Input your passcode on the device.

• Turn off the Lost Mode feature by taking the following steps:

1. Go to "Find My"

2. Select the device.

3. Go to Mark as Lost.

4. Tap Pending or Activated.

5. Tap on Turn Off Mark As Lost.

6. Tap Turn Off.

Unlock a Mac

• Once you find your lost Mac, you will need to input the numeric passcode on the device to get it unlocked. The Numeric passcode is the code that was set up when your Mac was marked as lost.

• In case you have forgotten your passcode, it can be recovered by using Find My iPad 8 Gen on iCloud.com.

• Once you lose your iPad 8 Gen, it is advisable to turn on the Lost Mode making use of the Find My iPad 8 Gen on iCloud.com.

Erasing a device in Find My on iPad 8 Gen

• The Find My app can be used in erasing an iPad 8 Gen, iPod touch, iPad 8 Gen, Apple Watch, or Mac.

• The Find My [device] must be turned on before losing your device for you to remotely erase the device.

What Happens When A Device Is Erased In Find My?

• You will receive a confirmation email on your Apple ID email address.

• When the iPad 8 Gen, iPod touch, iPad 8 Gen or Apple Watch is remotely erased using the Find My app, it will remain protected by the Activation Lock. To reactivate, you will need to re-enter your Apple ID and password.

• Once a device has been erased, you will not be able to employ the use of the Find My in locating the device or play sound on it.

Nevertheless, if near a previously used Wi-Fi network, you may still be able to locate your Mac or Apple Watch.

• The Apple Pay feature will be disabled for your device. Information on your credit or debit cards that have been set up for Apple Pay including students ID cards and Express Transit cards will be removed from your device.

The credit, debit and student cards will be removed even if your device is in the offline mode while the Express Transit cards will wait till your device go online to be removed as well.

Erasing a Device

1. Go to the Devices list.

2. Tap the Device to be erased.

3. Select Erase This Device.

4. Tap Erase This [device]. Enter a passcode to lock if the device is a Mac and note that you will be required to use the passcode to get it unlocked the next time you want to.

5. There may be a need for you to enter a phone number and message for you to be reached if the device is lost Both the number and message will be displayed on the device's lock screen.

6. Tap Erase.

7. Input your Apple ID password.

8. Tap Erase again.

Note that if the device is in the offline mode, the remote erase will begin the next time it gets connected to Wi-Fi or cellular network.

Canceling an Erase

If a device which was lost and erased when offline was found before it comes back online, the erase request can be canceled by taking the following steps:

1. Go to the Devices list.
2. Select the erased device you want to cancel.
3. Tap Cancel Erase.
4. Input your Apple ID password.

Note: A lost iPad 8 Gen can be erased by making use of the Find My iPad 8 Gen on iCloud.com.

Adjust Map Settings in Find My On iPad 8 Gen

- The map view or distance units can be changed in the Find My app.
- However, these settings will only affect maps available in the Find My app on the device but will not affect maps found in other apps or other devices.

Changing map view

1. Go to the top right corner of the map.
2. Tap the Map Settings button.
3. Below the Map View.

4. You can select Map, Hybrid, or Satellite.

Changing distance units

1. Go to the top right corner of the map.

2. Tap the Map Settings button.

3. Select Miles or Kilometers below the Distance option.

Chapter 15: Add and Use the Contact Information on iPad 8 Gen

You can check and modify your contacts from private, corporate, and other accounts in the Contacts app. You can also establish contacts and design a contact card with your own data.

Ask Siri. You can speak commands such as:

- "Where does my sister work?"
- "Aaliyah is my nephew"
- "Send a text to Aaliyah"

Create a Contact

Siri can also suggest fresh contacts depending on your use of other applications, like receiving notification in Mail and Calendar invites. You can otherwise switch off this function, from Settings > Contacts > Siri & Search and then switch off Show Siri Suggestions for contacts.

Siri also offers suggestions for contact data in other applications depending on how you've been using Contacts. To switch this function off, from Settings go to Contacts > Siri & Search, and switch off Learn from this App.

Find A Contact

Click the search area by the top of your list of contacts and register the name, address, telephone digits or any other contact details.

Share a Contact

Click on a name in your contact list, and press Share Contact, then select the procedure to send the details.

When you press Share Contact it transfers every detail you entered on the contact card.

Quickly Reach a Contact

To enter a text, create a mobile call or call through FaceTime, write an email or transfer funds through Apple Pay, press a key under the title of the contact.

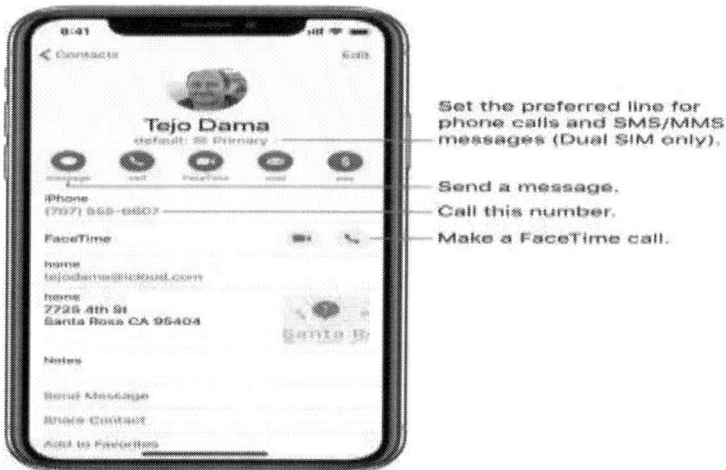

To modify the standard telephone digits or an email address for a contact mode, long-press the key under the contact title for that technique, and click on your choice in the list.

Delete A Contact

1. Navigate to the contact's card, and press Edit.

2. Flick to the bottom and select Delete Contact.

Edit Contacts on iPad 8 Gen

Attach a picture to a person in the Contacts, alter a tag, attach a birthdate, et.c

1. Click on a contact, and press Edit.

2. Execute any of the actions listed below:

- Attach a picture to someone in your contacts: click "Add photo." You could snap a picture or attach a picture from the device.
- Alter a label: press label, and pick one out of the list or click Add Custom Label to generate your own tag.
- Add an anniversary, social image, related title, et.c: press the Add key next to the object.
- Enable contact calls or SMS to negate the Do not disturb: press Ring or Text Tone, and switch on Emergency Bypass.
- Click on the Notes field to enter Notes.
- Attach a phonetic title, prefix and more: press the add field and pick an object from the menu.
- Click the Delete tab next to a contact, to remove a Contact's details.

3. When done, click Done.

If you call or message a particular contact on versions that come with a Dual SIM, your iPad 8 Gen utilizes the same path you used to communicate with that person automatically. To pick a chosen SIM for telephone calls and messages, choose your contact, press the default tab below the title of that contact and pick a SIM.

To alter the arrangements of your phone contacts, from Settings go to Contacts.

Add your contact info on iPad 8 Gen

Attach your details to your iPad 8 Gen contact card through the contacts application. iPad 8 Gen incorporates your Apple ID into your My Card feature which is your contact card, but you'll need to fill in your personal data like title and address.

Complete My Card

Click on My Card at the upper corner of your list of contacts, and click Edit. Contacts can propose mobile digits or addresses to assist in setting up My Card.

Click Add key if there isn't My Card, after which you're to submit your data.

From Settings go to Contacts > My Info and click your signature in the list of Contacts.

Edit My Card

Click on **My card** at the upper corner of your list of contacts and press Edit.

Create or edit your Medical ID

Click My Card at the upper edge of the contacts, click Edit, swipe down the screen to press Create Medical ID or and Edit Medical ID.

Use other contact accounts on iPad 8 Gen

The Contacts tool allows you to add people from other sources.

Use your iCloud contacts

Switch Contacts on and go to Settings > [your name] > iCloud

Use your Google contacts

1. From Settings go to Passwords & Accounts.

2. Click on Google, log in to your Google account, and switch Contacts on.

Add Contacts from another Account

1. From Settings go to Passwords & Accounts > Add Account.

2. Select and log in to an account, and switch Contacts on.

Access a Microsoft Exchange Global Address List

1. From Settings go to Passwords & Accounts.

2. Click Exchange, log in to your account there and switch Contacts on.

Set up an LDAP or CardDAV account to access business or school directories

1. From Settings go to Passwords & Accounts > Add Account > Other.

2. Press Add LDAP Account or Add CardDAV Account, and type in your details.

Sync Contacts from Your Computer Using iTunes

Through the iTunes software on your PC, tap **Info** in your PC's info field, and click Sync Contacts.

Download contacts from a SIM card (GSM)

From Settings go to Contacts > Import SIM Contacts.

Import Contacts from A Vcard

In an email or text, click a.vcf attachment. Add a contact from a directory

1. Click Groups, and press the folder you want to check for GAL, LDAP or CarDAV.

2. Press Done, and type your search in the field.

3. Press the name of the person to save in your contacts.

Show or Hide A Group

Click on Groups, and pick the groups you'll like to check. This key will only show if you have more than one contact base.

You can call contacts in the iPad 8 Gen phone app and attach new or current callers.

Add a Favorite

Place VIP contacts for fast phoning in your Favorites page.

Choose a contact, swipe down and click on Add to Favorites.

Phoning people from the favorites page is not hindered by Do Not Disturb.

Save the number you just dialed

1. Press Keypad to input a person's details into the phone app, and touch Add Number.

2. Click Create New Contact, or Add to Contact, and pick a contact.

Add a recent caller to Contacts

1. Click Recents in the phone app and add More Info next to the contact.

2. Click Create New Contact, or Add to Contact, and pick a number.

Automate Dialing an Extension or Passcode

If the contact you call needs an extension to be dialed, it can be filled for you by iPad 8 Gen. Tap the Symbols key when changing the digits of contact, and execute any below:

- To type in a 2-second pause, press Pause. A comma is used to represent a 2-second delay in a number
- Click on Wait to end a call till you're-click Call. Wait-to-dial is depicted in the contact as a semicolon.

Hide Duplicate Contacts on iPad 8 Gen

In the Contact application, link the same person's contact cards in various accounts so they'll show up only once in the All Contacts. You might have numerous submissions for the same individual if you have contacts from various outlets.

Phone numbers from distinct sites with the same name are connected and presented as a single coherent contact to prevent unnecessary records from occurring inside your list of contacts. The label Unified occurs when you access a unified phone number.

Link contacts

When 2 submissions are not automatically connected to that same person, you can link them by yourself.

1. Click on a phone number, press Edit, and click on Link Contacts.

2. To connect to some other phone number register, click Link.

The names on the contact cards do not change when you connect phone numbers with distinct first or last names. only the initial name shows on the unified card. Click on one of the related cards to select the name that displays on the unified card, click the name of the contact and press Use This Name Unified Card.

Bear in mind that connected contacts will not be combined. If you alter or attach data to a unified contact, the modifications will be transferred to each origin file where they are already.

Chapter 16: Set up FaceTime on iPad 8 Gen

You can create clip or audio calls to loved ones with your FaceTime app, whether they use an iPad 8 Gen, iPod touch, iPad 8 Gen or a Mac. You could speak face-to-face with the frontal camera; move to the back camera to send what's in your environment. Take a FaceTime Live Picture to shoot a Gif of your talks.

Keep in mind that there may be limits to FaceTime functions in some locations.

1. From Settings go to FaceTime, and switch FaceTime on.

2. Switch on FaceTime Live Photos if you want Live Photos while FaceTiming

3. To utilize the FaceTime function fill in your phone digits, Apple ID or email.

Make and Receive Facetime Calls on iPad 8 Gen

Making and receiving calls with the FaceTime is possible once you have Internet access and an Apple ID (firstly you should log in with your Apple ID or sign up for it if you don't have one).

You can always use your mobile data to make a call with Facetime, but this might cause extra charges. From Settings go to Cellular and switch Facetime off if you don't want this feature.

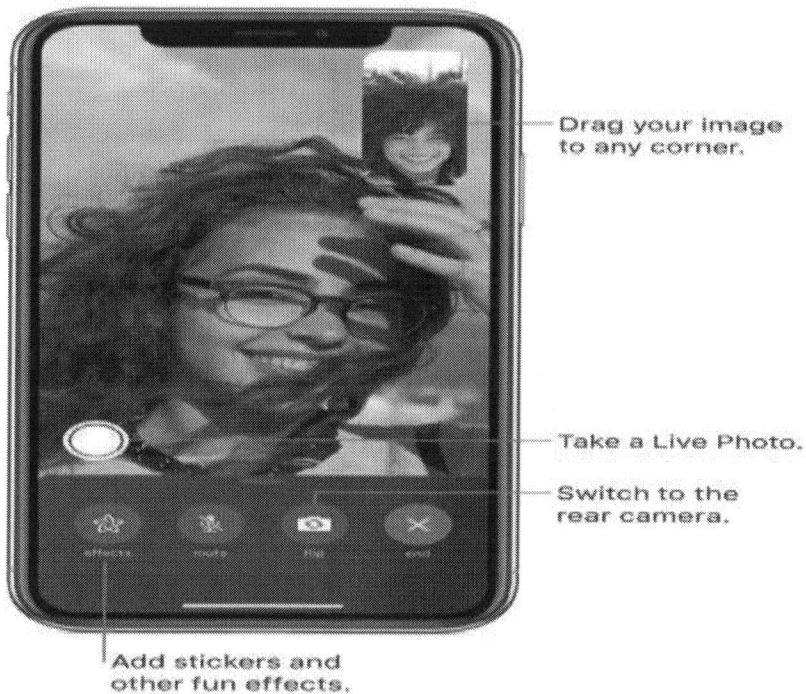

Drag your image to any corner.

Take a Live Photo.

Switch to the rear camera.

Add stickers and other fun effects.

Make a Facetime Call

Ask Siri. Speak a command like: "call with Facetime."

1. From FaceTime, Press Add tab at the upper right corner of the screen,

2. In the entry area on top of the screen, type in the digits or name you want to dial and click Video or Audio to create a video or audio call.

Note: not all locations support making a FaceTime audio call.

You could also press the Add Contact tab to launch Contacts and begin your dial-up instantly or click on a phone number from your FaceTime call list for fast dialing.

Hint: Flip iPad 8 Gen around to utilize the landscape orientation feature so as to be able to capture more while on a Facetime video call.

Leave a message

If nobody responds to your call from FaceTime, execute whichever of the steps below:

- Click on Leave a Message.
- To cancel a dial press Cancel.
- To dial back press Call Back

Start A Facetime Call From A Messages Conversation

A FaceTime call to someone you're texting is possible through Message conversation.

1. Click the profile image, My Account tab, or the name of the person you're chatting in Messages conversation.

2. Click on FaceTime.

Call again

Click on the details of a contact in the call history section or press the Info key to select a phone number in Contacts, from there you may begin your dial-up.

Receive A Facetime Call

If you receive a FaceTime call, Press any of the tabs below:

- Accept to pick the call.
- Decline to reject a call.

- Remind Me to fix a call back alert
- Message for Sending either SMS or MMS to your caller.

You may press either the End & Accept or Hold & Accept tabs if you are on a different call and a FaceTime caller rings you.

Delete A Call From Your Call History

From the FaceTime, flick to the left on top the contacts call history and click on Delete.

Make a Group FaceTime call on iPad 8 Gen

You can invite as much as 32 participants to a FaceTime group call with the FaceTime feature.

 Note: not allowed in some locations.

Start a Group FaceTime call

1. From FaceTime, click the Add tab in the upper right corner.

2. Then in the top of the entry area, you can write the digits or initials of the contacts you'll like to dial.

Also, you may add people to the group from your contacts list by clicking on the Add Contact tab.

3. You can either press Video or Audio to create a Facetime video or audio calls respectively.

Every contact is displayed in a different tile, and the bigger tiles revealing the members who are more active.

Every member is displayed in a tile. Whenever a contact talks or you press the pane, it shifts forward and becomes prevalent. Panes that can not fit are automatically displayed below the screen in a row. Scroll the rows to find the contact that you want to view. (Unless an image is available, the name or number of the contact will only be shown)

Start a Group Facetime Call from a Group Messages Conversation

You can launch a Group FaceTime dial with everyone you chat within the group's Messages conversation.

1. Click the profile images or tap the My Account tab on top of the chats in Messages conversation.

2. Press FaceTime.

Add another Person to a Call

Through a Group FaceTiming, any participant can add another individual whenever they want.

1. Click the phone display to operate the controls while FaceTiming. Scroll from above the controls, and click on Add Person.

2. Enter into the top entry section, the name, Apple ID, or phone digits of the person you want to include in the group

Or Press the Add tab To add a person from your contact list.

3. Press the Add to include someone in FaceTime

Join a Group Facetime Call

If you are invited by someone to join their group on Facetime, you'll see the incoming call and if you reject the call, they'll get notified. But with a click, you can accept the call and be part of the Facetime group.

Block unwanted callers in FaceTime on iPad 8 Gen

You can decide to block voice calls, text message and FaceTime calls from unwanted callers using the FaceTime app. To do this:

1.. Head to Settings > FaceTime > Blocked Contacts.

2. Then Scroll down, and tap Add New below the list.

3. Choose a contact you'd like to block.

To have a phone number or contact unblocked, swipe it to the left and then tap unblock.

Chapter 17: Collecting Health and Fitness Data on iPad 8 Gen

The Health app is very useful in tracking your daily footsteps including the flights of stairs you climb. Other data such as your body weight and caffeine intake can be manually added as well as tracking additional data with other apps such as nutrition and fitness apps including devices that are compatible with health such as AirPods, Apple Watch, weight scales, and blood pressure monitors.

Manually Updating Your Health Profile

At the initial opening of the Health app, you will be asked to set up your health profile to include basic information such as your date of birth and sex. If this information is not included when the health app is set up, you can get to update it later by taking the following steps:

1. Go to the top right of the Summary screen.
2. Tap your profile picture.
3. Tap Summary at the lower left in case you don't see your profile picture.
4. Select Health profile.
5. Tap Edit.

6. Tap a field to make a change.

7. Tap Done.

Manually Adding Data to A Health Category

1. Go to the bottom right.

2. Tap Browse to display the Health Categories screen.

3. Then perform one of the following actions.

- Tap a category: Scroll down to see all the categories available.

- Tap the search field and input the name of a category such as body measurements or specific data types such as weight.

4. Select the Details button for the data you like to update.

5. Go to the top right corner of the screen.

6. Tap Add Data.

7. Input your information.

8. Go to the top right corner of the screen.

9. Tap Add or Done.

Collecting data from other sources

• From Apple Watch: A periodic heart rate measurement will be automatically sent from the Apple watch to Health after pairing your iPad 8 Gen with Apple Watch. The Apple Watch can also be configured to send activity metrics, noise levels, etc, to Health.

• From headphones: Your headphones' audio levels will be automatically sent to Health after connecting Earpods, Airpods as well as other compatible headphones to your iPad 8 Gen.

• From an app that is downloaded from the App Store: You can allow the app to share data with Health while setting up the app.

• From another device: Here you will need to follow the setup instructions for such a device.

• Note that if the device is a Bluetooth device, you will need to get it paired with the iPad 8 Gen.

WARNING: Both iPad 8 Gen and Apple Watch are not medical devices. **Viewing** Health and Fitness Information on iPad 8 Gen

With the Health app, you can easily get access to your health and fitness information.

Viewing your highlights

1. Go to the lower left.

2. Tap Summary.

3. Scroll down to see the highlights of your recent health and fitness data.

4. Tap the Details button to see more details about a category.

Adding or removing a health category from Favorites on the Summary screen

1. Go to the lower left.

2. Tap Summary.

3. Select Edit for the Favorites section.

4. Tap a category to get it turned on or off.

5. Tap Done.

Viewing Details in the Health Categories

1. Go to the bottom right.

2. Tap Browse to display the Health Categories screen.

3. Perform one of the following actions:

- Tap a category: Scroll down or up to see all categories.

- Tap the search field and input the name of the category such as Nutrition or a specific data types such as Protein.

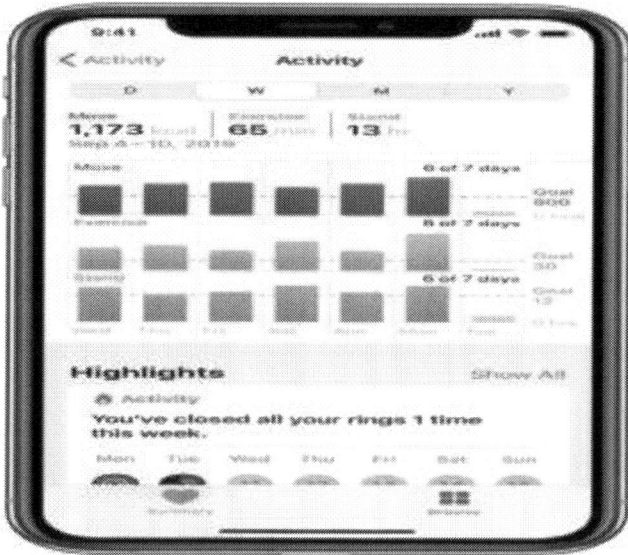

Tap the Details button to view details about any of the data. You can get to do any of the following depending on the data type:

- See weekly, monthly, and yearly views of the data: Go to the top screen and tap the tabs.

- Manually entering data: Go to the top right corner of the screen and tap Add Data.

- Moving a data type to favorites on the Summary screen: Get the "Add to Favorites" turned on. In case you do not see the Add to Favorites option, scroll downwards.

• View which apps and devices are allowed to share data: Go below Options and tap Data Sources & Access. If you don't see Options, scroll downwards to access it.

Delete data: To do this, take the following steps:

1. Tap Show All Data below Options.

2. Swipe to the left on the data record.

3. Tap Delete.

4. Delete All data by selecting Edit and Tapping Delete All.

Change the measurement unit: Select Unit below Options and choose a different unit.

Learn more about health and fitness

• Introductory articles, app suggestions, and other information are found at the bottom of the Summary screen. Tap an item for more information.

• Many categories also show recommended apps when you view health categories details.

Tracking Your Menstrual Cycle on iPad 8 Gen

You can track your menstrual cycle to get information about period and fertility predictions in the Health app.

Getting started with cycle tracking

1. Go to the bottom right of the Health app.

2. Tap Browse.

3. Select Cycle Tracking.

Note: You can improve information about your period and fertility window by entering the requested information about your last period.

Logging Your Cycle Information

1. Go to the bottom right of the Health app.

2. Tap Browse.

3. Select Cycle Tracking.

4. Then perform any of the following actions:

• **Log a period day:** Select a day in the timeline available at the top of the screen. Tap Period below Cycle Log to log the flow level for that day and select an option. Alternatively, go to the top right and tap Add Period then select days from the monthly calendar. Note that the logged days are marked on the timeline using solid red circles. Tap a logged day to get it removed.

• **Log symptoms:** To select a day, drag the timeline at the top of the screen, tap Symptoms and then select all that apply.

Tap Done when you have finished. Note that days with symptoms are indicated with purple dots.

• Log spotting: To select a day, drag the timeline, tap Spotting, select Had Spotting and then select Done.

5. For additional categories to be added such as ovulation test results and basal body temperature, tap Options and select the categories.

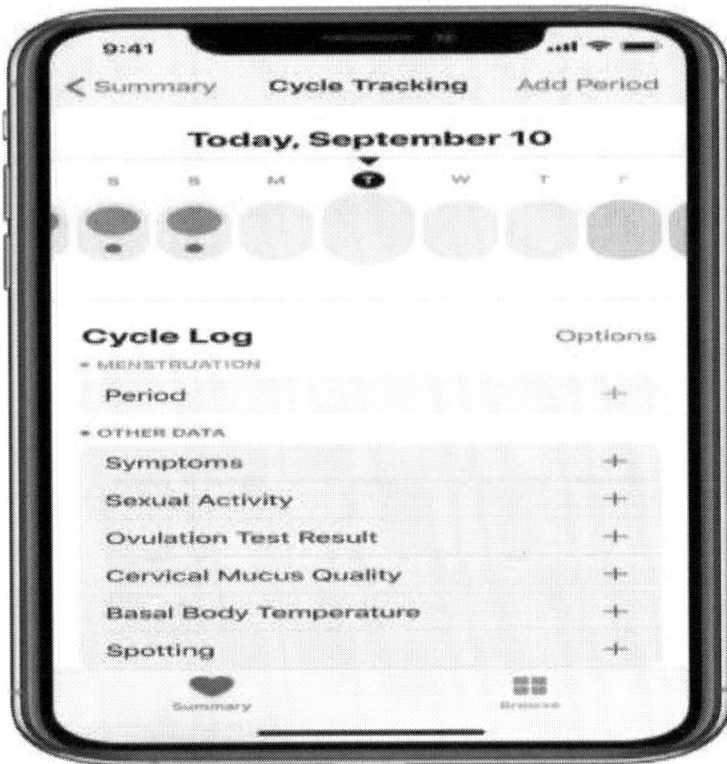

Viewing the cycle timeline

1. Go to the bottom right of the Health app.

2. Tap Browse.

3. Select Cycle Tracking.

The Timeline information is displayed using the following format:

- Solid red circles: This indicates days you logged for your period.

- Purple dots: This indicates days you logged for having symptoms.

- Light red circles: This is used to indicate your period prediction. Tap Options and turn on or off, Period Prediction to hide or show predicted period days.

• Light blue days: This is used to indicate a prediction of your likely fertility window. This should be used as a form of birth control. Hide or show the fertile window prediction by tapping on Options and turning the Fertility Prediction on or off.

To have different days selected, drag the timeline. The data that you logged for the selected day will appear below the Cycle Log.

Changing the Period and Fertility Notifications and Other Cycle Tracking Options

1. Go to the bottom right of the Health app.
2. Tap Browse.
3. Select Cycle Tracking.
4. Scroll down and tap Options.
5. Turn an option on or off by tapping it.

Viewing your cycle history and statistics

1. Go to the bottom right of the Health app.
2. Tap Browse.
3. Select Cycle Tracking.

4. To see the timelines of your three most recent periods, scroll downwards.

5. Scroll further to see related statistics.

6. Tap the Details button, to see more details including older information for Cycle History or Statistics.

To find days matching a particular symptom or flow level in the detailed Cycle History:

1. Go to the top right.

2. Tap Filters.

3. Select an Option.

4. Tap Done.

Chapter 18: Use the Home App on iPad 8 Gen

You are provided with a secure way of controlling and automating HomeKit-enabled accessories such as lights, locks, smart TVs, etc, with the use of the Home app. The Home apps also enable you to control any work with Apple HomeKit accessory with the use of your iPad 8 Gen.

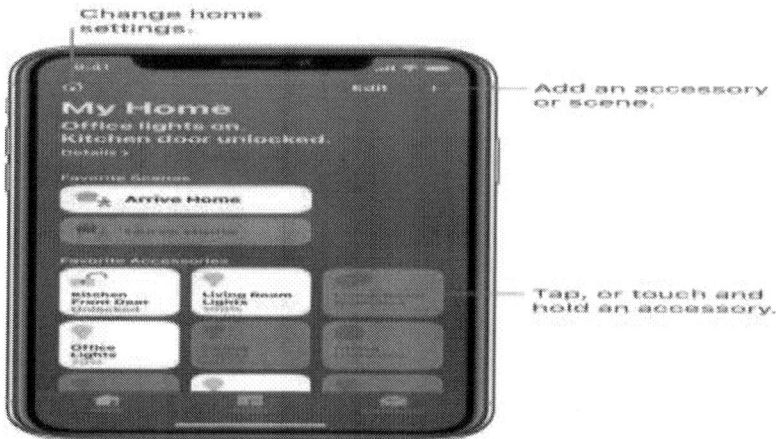

• Accessories can be controlled individually after setting up your home and its rooms. You can also make use of scenes in controlling multiple accessories with the use of one command. An example is creating a scene called "wake up" which will then turn on the lights in the kitchen, unlocks the front door and raises the thermostat.

• The Apple TV of the 4th generation or later, HomePod or iPad 8 Gen with the iOS 10.3, iPad 8 GenoS 13 or later can all be used in controlling your home automatically and remotely with the mentioned devices left at home.

• Scenes can be scheduled to run automatically at certain times or a particular accessory can be activated such as unlocking the front door of your home.

• These features also enable you as well as others that you invited to securely control your home even when you are away.

Set up Accessories with Home App on iPad 8 Gen

• At the initial opening of the Home App, the setup assistant guides you on creating a home where accessories can be added and you will also get to define each room.

• If a home has already been created making use of another HomeKit-enabled app, then this step will be skipped.

Adding an Accessory to Home

• Make sure the accessory you are adding such as light or camera is connected to a power source and turned on.

• Also, ensure that it is connected to your Wi-Fi network.

Once you have followed the above instructions, you are then required to take the following steps:

1. Select the Home tab.

2. Tap the Add button.

3. Tap Add Accessory.

4. Follow the onscreen instructions.

Note

• Once an accessory is added, it will be assigned to a default room or a room that is chosen by you.

• There may be a need for you to scan a QR code or input in an 8-digit HomeKit setup code which can be found on the accessory to be added or its documentation or box.

• For a supported smart TV, the QR code is displayed for you to scan.

• The accessory can be assigned to a room and given a name. The name can then be used in controlling the accessory with Siri.

Create and Use Scenes in Home On iPad 8 Gen

Scenes can be created to allow the control of multiple accessories at once in the Home app. An example is defining a "Reading" scene that can be used to adjust lights, close the drapes and get the thermostat adjusted.

Create a Scene

1. Tap the Home tab.
2. Select the Add button.
3. Tap on Add Scene.
4. Tap Custom.
5. Input a name for the scene.
6. Tap Add Accessories.
7. Select the accessories you want this scene to include.

8. Tap Done. The first accessory that is selected is used in determining the room the scene is assigned to. Selecting the bedroom lamp, for example, means that the scene is assigned to your bedroom.

9. Lastly, set each of the accessories to the state you want it in when the scene is run.

Use Scenes

1. Tap the Rooms tab.

2. Tap on the Show Rooms button.

3. Select the room the scene is assigned to.

4. Then do one of the following

- Run a scene: Tap on the scene.

- Change a scene: Touch and hold a scene

The following can be done with the scene:

- Changing the scene's name.

- Test the scene.

- Add or remove accessories.

- Include the scene in the favorites. All favorites' scenes will appear in the Home tab.

Control Your Home Using Siri on iPad 8 Gen

Apart from using the Home app, Siri can be used in controlling your accessories and scenes. The following are things you can say to Siri for controlling the accessories that are added including the scenes, rooms or homes you set up:

- "Turn down the kitchen lights"
- "Turn off the lights in the Chicago house"
- "Turn off the lights" or "Turn on the lights"
- "Did I lock the front door?"
- "Set the temperature to 68 degrees"
- "Set my reading scene"

Organize Rooms into Zones

To easily control different areas of your home using Siri, have the rooms grouped into a zone. To do this you are required to take the following steps:

1. Tap Rooms.
2. Tap on Show Rooms button.
3. Tap on Room Settings.
4. Select a room.
5. Tap Zone.
6. Select an "existing zone" or tap on "Create New" to add the room to a new zone.

Editing a Room

A room's name and wallpaper can be changed, get the room added to a zone or delete the room. Once a room is removed, the accessories that are assigned to it will be automatically moved to a Default Room. To get your room edited, you are required to take the following steps:

1. Tap Rooms.

2. Tap on Show Rooms button.

3. Select Room Settings.

4. Tap a room.

Set up HomePod in Home on iPad 8 Gen

The Home app can be used to add and edit alarms on HomePod as well as controlling many of its settings.

Using Home in adding and editing HomePod alarms

1. Go to the Home app.

2. Touch the HomePod button and hold it.

3. Swipe up or tap the Settings button.

4. Tap Alarms.

5. Then do any of the following:

Add an alarm:

1. Tap the Add button.

2. Create an alarm.

3. Tap Save.

Edit an alarm:

1. Tap Edit.

Chapter 19: Monitoring the Audio Levels on iPad 8 Gen

The health app can be used in monitoring the audio levels from headphones and sound levels from your environment. It helps you to understand how long and often you are being exposed to loud volume to prevent it from affecting your hearing.

View audio levels

- Once EarPods, AirPods, and other compatible headphones are connected to your iPad 8 Gen, the audio levels will be automatically sent to Health.
- After pairing your Apple Watch with your iPad 8 Gen and the Noise app is set up on your Apple Watch (watchOS 6 required), the environmental sound levels will be automatically sent from your Apple Watch to Health.
- It is to be noted that measurements are accurate from Airpods when compared to the headphones when connected by wire. The wired headphone measurements are estimated based on the volume of your iPad 8 Gen.

1. Go to the bottom right.
2. Tap Browse.
3. Tap Hearing
4. Select Headphone Audio Levels or Environmental Sound Levels.
5. Then you can now do any of the following:

- Learn about sound level classifications: Do this by tapping the Show Information button.

- View exposure levels over some time: Tap the tabs located at the top of the screen. It is to be noted that all levels are measured in decibels.

- Change the period displayed in the graph: Swipe the graph to the left or right.

- See details about a moment in time: Do this by touching and holding the graph then drag to move the selection.

- View details about average exposure: Select Show All Filters and tap Daily Average.

- View a line representing average exposure: Tap on Exposure located below the graph.

- View the high and low range: Select Show All Filters and tap Range.

- Filter the data by headphones: To do this, tap Show All Filters and scroll to the bottom of the screen, then select one of your headphones.

- View highlights: Scroll downwards to see more and tap Show All.

Viewing Noise Notifications for Environmental Sounds

When sounds are over 80 decibels, they can be considered as generally loud. The Apple Watch is designed such that you will get notified once the sound gets to a level that may harm your hearing.

Go to the bottom right.

1. Tap Browse.
2. Tap Hearing.
3. Select Noise Notifications.
4. Tap a notification to see more details.

Health and Fitness Data on iPad 8 Gen

• Other apps can be given permission to share health and fitness data using the Health app. When a workout app is installed, for example, the Health app can help in displaying its exercise data.

• The workout app can also read and use data shared by other devices and apps such as heart rate and weight.

Control the Sharing Of Data among Apps and Devices

1. Go to the top right.
2. Tap your profile picture.
3. Tap Summary or Browse at the bottom of the screen if you don't see a profile picture, then scroll to the top of the screen.
4. Tap Apps or Devices below Privacy. The screen will then list the items that requested access to Health data.
5. Change the access to an item by tapping it.
6. Turn on or off permission to write data to Health.

Export and Share Your Health Data

1. Go to the top right.

2. Tap your profile picture.

3. Tap Summary or Browse at the bottom of the screen if you don't see a profile picture, then scroll to the top of the screen.

4. Select Export all health data.

5. Select a method for sharing your data.

Note that your data will be exported in the XML format which is a common format used for sharing data between apps.

Download Health Records in Health On iPad 8 Gen (The U.S. Only)

- With the Health app, you can access information from supported health organizations regarding your conditions, allergies, medications, etc.

- Once you make use of the passcode, Touch ID, or Face ID in locking your iPad 8 Gen, all the health data available in your Health app will be encrypted except what was added to your Medical ID.

Set up Automatic Downloads

1. Go to the top right.

2. Tap your profile picture.

3. Select Health Records.

4. Tap Summary or Browse at the bottom of the screen if you don't see a profile picture, then scroll to the top of the page.

5. Then do one of the following:

- Set up your first download: Tap on Get Started.
- Set up downloads for additional accounts: Tap on Add Account.

6. Input the name of an organization e.g. clinic or hospital where your health records were obtained. Alternatively, you can find a list of nearby organizations and input the name of the city or state you live in.

7. Tap a result to open it.

8. Tap the Connect to Account button below the Available to Connect to navigate to the sign-in screen for your patient portal.

9. Input in the username and password that was used for the patient web portal of that organization.

10. Follow the onscreen instructions.

It is to be noted that your health organization might not be available for this feature. Organization information is frequently updated.

View your health records

1. Go to the bottom right.

2. Tap Browse to display the Health Categories screen.

3. Then perform one of the following actions:

- Tap on the search field and input the name of a health record category such as Clinical Vitals or a data type such as Blood pressure.

- Scroll down and select a category such as Allergies or Clinical Vitals below the Health Records

- Scroll down and tap the name of a particular organization.

4. Tap any section having the Details button for more details.

Customizing Notification Settings for Health Records

1. Go to Settings.

2. Tap Notifications.

3. Tap Health.

4. Select Options.

Delete an organization and its records from iPad 8 Gen

1. Go to the top right.

2. Tap your profile picture.

3. Tap Health Records.

4. Tap Summary or Browse at the bottom of the screen if you don't see a profile picture, then scroll to the top of the page.

5. Tap on the name of an organization.

6. Tap Remove Account.

Sharing Your Records with Other Apps

You can be asked by third-party apps for your health records to be viewed. Before access is granted to such a third-party, ensure that the app is trusted with your records.

1. To grant access, select which categories to be shared when prompted. Examples of categories include allergies, medications, or immunization.

2. Choose whether access should be granted to your current and future health records or just your current records. If only your current records are chosen to be shared, you will be asked to grant access whenever new records are being downloaded to your iPad 8 Gen.

Turn off the permission to read data from Health to stop sharing health records with the app.

Creating a Medical ID in Health on iPad 8 Gen

Critical medical and contact information can be supplied for first responders and others who have access to your iPad 8 Gen using the Health app.

By simply tapping on Emergency and then Medical ID from the Lock screen, they will be able to access your Medical ID without having to enter a Passcode.

Setting up your Medical ID

1. Go to the top right.
2. Tap your profile picture.
3. Tap Summary or Browse at the bottom of the screen if you don't see a profile picture, then scroll to the top of the screen.

4. Select Medical ID.

5. Tap Get Started.

Reviewing or Changing Your Medical ID

1. Go to the top right.

2. Tap your profile picture.

3. Tap Summary or Browse at the bottom of the screen if you don't see a profile picture, then scroll to the top of the screen.

4. Select Medical ID.

5. Tap Edit to make changes.

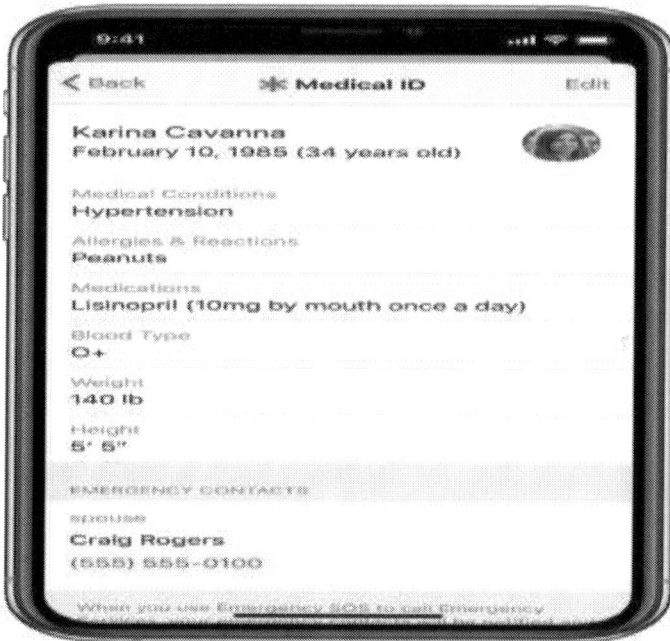

TIP: Your Medical ID can be quickly viewed from the Home screen by touching and holding the Health app icon and selecting Medical ID.

Prevent viewing from the Lock screen

1. Go to the top right.

2. Tap your profile picture.

3. Select Medical ID.

4. Tap Edit.

5. Turn off Show When Locked.

6. Tap Summary or Browse at the bottom of the screen if you don't see a profile picture, then scroll to the top of the page.

View Your Medical ID from The Lock Screen

To view how your Medical ID is displayed to emergency responders, you can do any of the following:

1. Press and hold the side button and either of the Volume buttons till the sliders come up.

2. Drag the slider for Medical ID.

3. Tap Done.

Note that the next time you get your iPad 8 Gen unlocked, your passcode will be required to enable the Face ID feature again.

Register as an organ donor in Health on iPad 8 Gen (U.S. Only)

- With the Health app, you can register to be an organ, tissue, or eye donor with Donate Life America.

- Once you decide to donate, it becomes accessible to others in your Medical ID.

- If you change your decision to donate, you can simply have your registration removed.

Learn About Organ Donation

1. Go to the top right.

2. Tap your profile picture.

3. Tap Summary or Browse at the bottom of the screen if you don't see a profile picture, then scroll to the top of the page.

4. Select Organ Donation.

5. Tap Learn More for an overview of organ donation and Donate Life America.

Registering with Donate Life America

1. Go to the top right.

2. Tap your profile picture.

3. Tap Organ Donation.

4. Tap Summary or Browse at the bottom of the screen if you don't see a profile picture, and then scroll to the top of the page.

5. Select Sign Up with Donate Life.

To alter your donor information or get your registration removed, you are required to take the following steps:

1. Tap your profile picture.

2. Tap Organ Donation.

3. Tap Edit Donor Registration.

Backing up your Health data on iPad 8 Gen

- Your health and fitness information in the Health app is automatically stored in the iCloud once you are signed in using your Apple ID.

- As your information goes between the iCloud and your device, they will be encrypted and stored in the iCloud.

- Your Health data can also be backed up by getting an iTune backup encrypted whether you are making use of the iCloud or not.

Stop Storing Your Health Data in iCloud

1. Go to Settings.
2. Tap [your name].
3. Select iCloud.
4. Turn off Health.

Chapter 20: How to Answer or Decline Incoming Calls on iPad

Your new iPad allows you to receive and make calls by relaying calls via your iPad.

If you want to use this method to make calls, you must setup FaceTime and use your Apple ID to sign on both iPhone and iPad device.

You have setup your iPhone and iPad device to allow phone calls on your iPad via your iPhone. To do this:

1. Go to Settings ⚙ > Cellular on your iPhone
2. Then choose a line (below Cellular Plans) if your iPhone has Dual SIM.
3. Then do any of the following:
   o You can Tap Calls on Other Devices, then turn on Allow Calls on Other Devices.
   o After that, choose your iPad alongside other devices you wish to make and receive calls with.

These steps allow the iPad and other devices that you're signed in with the same Apple ID to conveniently receive and make calls when they're close to your iPhone and are connected to Wi-Fi.

- o After this, Tap Wi-Fi Calling, then have the Add Wi-Fi Calling turned on for the Other Devices.

This allows iPad and other devices where you're signed in with the same Apple ID to make and receive calls even when your iPhone isn't nearby.

This lets your iPad as well as other devices that are signed in with the same apple ID to receive and make calls even when your iPhone is not nearby.

4. After that, setup FaceTime, on your iPad and sign in using the same Apple ID that is the same with your iPhone.
5. Head to Settings > FaceTime, and then turn on FaceTime and Calls from iPhone. Turn on Wi-Fi calling if you are asked.

Make or receive a phone call on your iPad

- *Make a call*: You will have to tap a phone number in **Contacts**, FaceTime, Calendar, Messages, Spotlight or Safari. Or you can just open FaceTime, and enter a contact or a phone number, then tap 📞.
- *Receive a call*: Swipe or tap the notification to answer or ignore the call.

Chapter 21: Multitasking with "Picture in Picture" on iPad

If you wish to watch videos or do FaceTime call while you do something else on another app, the picture in picture feature allows you do that. Simply tap the Picture in Picture button when using face time or watching a clip. The video will be reduced to a side of your screen. You can do the following at this stage:

- Resize the video window: To enlarge, pinch open. To shrink it, pinch closed.
- Show and hide controls by tapping the video window.
- Move the video window by dragging it to another corner of the screen.
- Hide the video window by dragging it off the edges of the screen.
- Close the video window by tapping the Close button.

You can tap the Full Screen button in the small video window if you wish to return to your former video or FaceTime.

Chapter 22: How to Get Cycling Directions from Your Current Location in Maps on Ipad

In the Maps app , worry no more about cycling directions and landmarks. Eateries, shops, great places and all can be easily discovered from the map feature consisting roads, paths and different lanes.

Note that Cycling directions are available in selected regions only . Most especially in China and the United states.

To get started:

1. Start with a voice command like "Hey Siri, give me cycling directions to work."

- Touch your destination and direction, then the Cycle button or

- Touch and hold any spot of your choice on the map, touch Directions, then the Cycle button.

2. Tap Go .

3. Tap End to stop navigation.

Note: You have the option to avoid hills or busy roads before you tap Go. So, you can select other routes if you like. You can also see an overview map of your route in a list instead of viewing turn by turn.

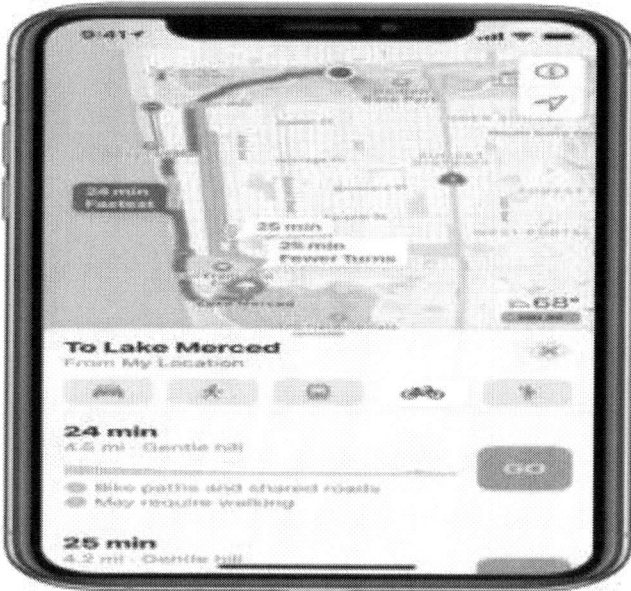

Explore new places with Guides in Maps on iPad

iPad has Guides from trusted partners that are automatically updated when new places are added in the Maps app. This is just to keep you up to date. You can discover great places to do various things with this feature. Guides are available in select regions. London and the United states especially.

To access one of the Guides, touch the search field, then;

- Below Editors' Picks, touch a cover that appears or
- Click See All, then at the top of the "All Guides card, select an option and tap a cover. Or
- Just swipe down, choose a publisher and tap a cover.

After that, you can:

- Save by tapping the Save Guide button.

- Share by tapping the Share button.

- Also add one of its destinations to My Guides by simply tapping the Add button, then select one of your available guides.

- Return to the search field by tapping the Close button.

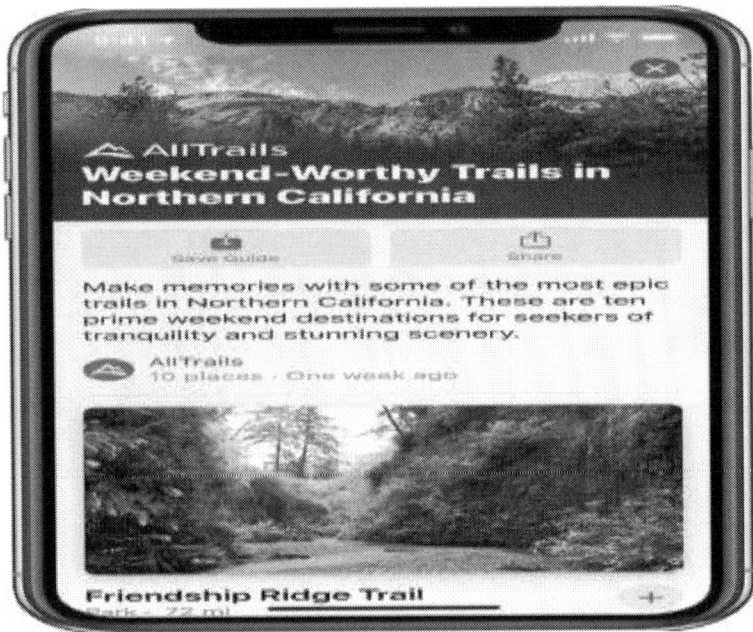

How to set up electric vehicle routing in Maps on iPad

If you wish to make stops for charging your electric vehicle, the map app can help you plan your trips. This however requires a compatible vehicle.

The first step is to install your vehicle's app on your iPad

Search for the vehicle manufacturer on App store and download the app that supports EV routing for your vehicle in particular. Open the app and follow its setup instructions.

To connect Maps to your vehicle's EV routing app,

1. Go to Settings button in Maps

2. Tap My Vehicles and click Connect Your Electric Vehicles.

3. Choose your vehicle name, then follow the remaining onscreen instructions.

When you're done, maps can track and analyze your vehicle charge and also identify appropriate charging stations on the way. It notifies you with the nearest station when your charge gets low.

To choose a different vehicle when you get directions

1. Get driving directions as instructed above.

2. Swipe the route card up before you tap Go.

3. Here, you can choose another electric vehicle

Chapter 23: How to record a QuickTake video

When you record a video in photo mode, it's called a QuickTake video.

To start recording a QuickTake video in Photo mode, Press and hold the volume up or down button. Then, tap the thumbnail to view the QuickTake video in the Photos app.

Alternatively,

1. When you're in Photo mode, touch and hold the Shutter button to start a QuickTake video.

2. You can also slide the Shutter button to the right and let go over the lock if you wish to perform a hands-free recording.To take a still photo while recording, tap the Shutter button that appears below the frame.

3. Touch the Record button again to stop recording.

How to record a slow-motion video

Any video done with this format is recorded normally but played with slow motion. You can also customize slow motion periods within a video by editing and choosing a desired time frame for the effect.

To get started, **Choose Slo-mo mode.**

1. Tap the Camera Chooser Back-Facing button if you wish to record in Slo-mo mode with the front camera.

2. Touch the Record button or press any volume button to start recording. Do same to stop.

To change slow-motion settings, go to Settings, click Camera and tap Record Slo-mo.

How to capture a time-lapse video

To create a time-lapse video such as a setting sun or flowing traffic by capturing footage at selected intervals,

1. Tap Time-lapse mode.

2. Put your iPad at a particular scene you wish to capture in motion.

3. Touch the Record button to start recording; do same to stop.

You can switch between the 1x zoom button and the 2x zoom button to zoom in for models with Dual and Triple camera system and between the 0.5x zoom button to zoom out iPad Pro.

When you take time-lapse 1080p video at 30 fps under low-light conditions on Auto Low Light FPS, iPad can automatically reduce the frame rate to 24 fps to improve the video quality. To do this, go to Settings, then Camera. Tap Record Video, and turn on Auto Low Light FPS.

How to use quick toggles to change video resolution and frame rate

To change video resolution and frame rates, use quick toggles in video mode.

In video mode, touch the quick toggles in the top-right corner to switch between HD or 4K recording and 24, 30, or 60 frames per second (fps).

To take a selfie;

To take a mirrored selfie that reflects front camera preview on, go to Settings, then Camera. Turn on Mirror Front Camera.

Touch the Camera Chooser Back-Facing button to switch to the front camera, While on all other models, tap the Camera Chooser Back-Facing button.

To increase the field of view, you'll see arrows inside the frame. Tap them and click the Shutter button or press any volume button to take the shot.

How to Pin A Conversation

- Tap the pin button after swiping right on the conversation or
- Drag the conversation to the top of the list by simply touching and holding.

How to unpin a conversation

You can also unpin conversations by doing any of these:

- Tap the unpin button after you touch and hold the conversation or
- Drag the conversation to the bottom of the list by simply touching and holding.

How to switch from a Message conversation to a FaceTime or audio call

If you wish to start a FaceTime or audio call with someone you're chatting with in messages app, you can do that by simply tapping the profile picture or the name of the person at the top of the conversation. Now, click FaceTime or audio.

To mention people in a conversation, Just type the contact's name in the text field and tap when it appears. You can also do this by typing "@" then the contact's name.

Go to Settings, then messages. Click notify me if you wish to change your own mention notification setting.

How to change a group name and photo

To put a personalized photo to a group conversation, tap the name or number at the top of the conversation, touch the "More Info" button at the top right, click Change Name and Photo, then choose any option you like.

How to use Business Chat

To get answers from businesses quickly, use the business chat option.

Note that: when you send business chat messages, it appears in dark gray. This is to differentiate them from messages sent using iMessage (in blue) and SMS/messages which appears green.

To get started with business chats,

1. Search for the business using any search app like Siri or maps.
2. Start a conversation by clicking a chat link in your search results.

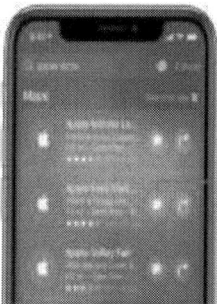

Tap here to start a conversation with this business.

How to reply to a specific message in a conversation

You can respond to a specific message inline by double-tapping (or touching and holding) the message, then touch the Reply button. Type your response and Send.

Index

Printed in Great Britain
by Amazon